Classroom
Atlas

Editor
Brett R. Gover

Research and Writing
Elizabeth Leppman, PhD

Cartographic Coordination
Nina Lusterman, Marzee Eckhoff

Cartography
Gregory P. Babiak, Rob Ferry, Marc Kugel

Design
Rand McNally Design

Copyright ©2013 RM Acquisition, LLC d/b/a Rand McNally
Rand McNally and the globe logo are registered trademarks of RM Aquisition, LLC.

Manufactured by RM Aquisition, LLC
9855 Woods Drive
Skokie, Illinois 60077

Printed in Madison, WI, U.S.A.
January 2015
3rd printing
PO# 32449
ISBN: 0-528-01025-5
ISBN-13: 978-0-528-01025-5

For information about ordering the *Classroom Atlas* or the *Classroom Atlas Teacher's Guide*, call 1-800-678-RAND (-7263) or visit our website at **www.randmcnally.com/education**.

Table of Contents

How to Use the Atlas

Getting to Know Your World

An atlas is a collection of maps. This atlas is a collection of more than 100 physical, political, and thematic maps. It also includes photographs, charts, graphs, and other special features.

Physical Maps

On the physical maps, different **land elevations** and **ocean depths** are shown by different colors. Major **physical features**, such as the Rocky Mountains in North America, and major rivers, such as the Colorado River, are named. Countries and some cities are also named.

Political Maps

The political maps show **political units**—areas under one government, such as countries, states, provinces, territories, and cities. Countries, states, and provinces are shown in different colors so that you can recognize them more easily. Cities are shown in different sizes of type and have different symbols to show their populations.

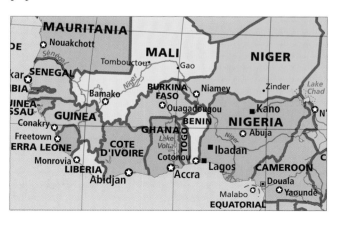

Map Legends

The **legend** of a map explains the symbols used on the map. It helps you "decode" the information. In this atlas, the legends on the physical and political maps explain much of the map information. To keep the legends on the individual maps from getting too large, these legends include only a few key symbols. The complete legend for all information on the physical and political maps is on page 7. Take some time to get familiar with these symbols so that you can recognize them on the individual maps.

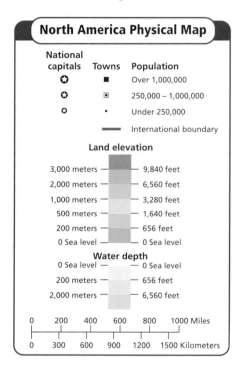

The **scale bar** in the legend tells how much smaller the map is than the real area it represents. The scale bar below is from the North America Political Map. To see how the scale bar works, place your ruler on the bar. You will see that one inch represents about 650 miles (one centimeter represents about 400 kilometers). Find two cities on the map that are about one inch apart (or two cities that are about one centimeter apart) on the North America Political Map. In the real world, these places are about 650 miles (or 400 kilometers) apart.

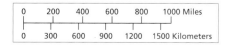

Directional Arrows

The physical and political maps in this atlas have directional arrows. The four arrows together are called a **compass rose**. The letters on the compass rose stand for **N**orth, **S**outh, **E**ast, and **W**est. On the map, the North arrow always points toward the North Pole. The South arrow always points toward the South Pole.

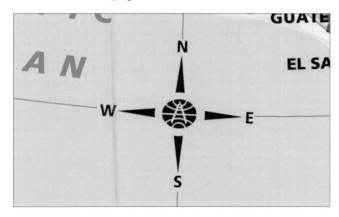

Map Grids

The blue lines drawn east-west across the maps are **lines of latitude**, or parallels. The blue lines drawn north-south are **lines of longitude**, or meridians. The lines of latitude and longitude create **grids** on the maps.

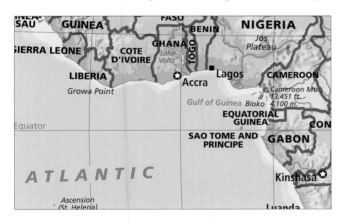

The physical and political maps have red letters along both sides and red numbers along the top and bottom. These letters and numbers are one way of giving names to these grids.

Look at the political map of Africa on page 87. Put your left index finger on the **E** at the left side of the map, and your right index finger on the **4** at the top of the map. Trace both fingers across the map until they meet at the grid square where the city of Lagos, Nigeria, is located.

Lagos is in the **E4** square of the grid on the map. The lines of latitude north and south of the E and the lines of longitude on either side of the 4 create the E4 square. (See the areas highlighted in purple on the map below.) E4 is the map key, or alpha-numeric grid location, for Lagos. What other cities are in the E4 square?

The city of Mogadishu in Somalia is in the E8 square. In what square do you find the country of Sierra Leone?

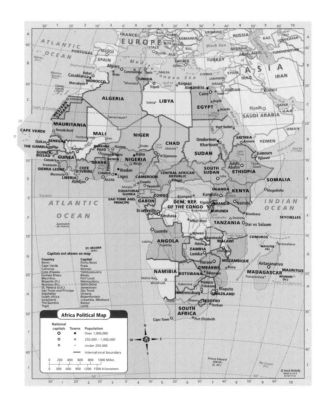

Index

The index is **a list in alphabetical order** of most of the places that appear on the maps. Each place entry in the index is followed by its map key, or alpha-numeric grid location, and the number of the page on which it appears.

Place	Map Key	Page
A		
Aberdeen, *South Dakota*	B6	**38**
Abidjan, *cap. Cote d'Ivoire, Afr.*	E3	**87**
Abilene, *Texas*	E6	**38**
Absaroka Range, *U.S.*	B3	**36**
Abu Dhabi, *cap. U.A.E., Asia*	C5	**99**
Abuja, *cap. Nigeria, Afr.*	E4	**87**
Acapulco, *Guerrero, Mexico*	C3	**64**
Accra, *cap. Ghana, Afr.*	E3	**87**
Aconcagua, *Cerro, highest peak,*		
S.A.	G4	**70**
Adana, *Turkey*	B3	**98**
Ad-Dammām, *Saudi Arabia*	C5	**98**
Addis Ababa, *cap. Ethiopia, Afr.*	E7	**87**
Adelaide, *cap. South Australia,*		
Austr.	D3	**111**

Place
Amundsen Sea, *A.*
Amur River, *Asia*
Anchorage, *Alaska*
Andaman Islands,
Andes, *mts., S.A.*
Andorra, *country,*
Angara River, *Rus.*
Angarsk, *Russia*
Angel Falls, *S.A.*
Angola, *country,*
Anguilla, *dep., N.*
Anhui, *province,*
Ankara, *cap. Turk*
Ann Arbor, *Michi*
Annapolis, *cap. M*
Anshan, *China*

Thematic Maps

Have you ever seen a weather map on television that uses different colors to show places with different temperatures? That map is a **thematic map**. It shows information about **a specific topic** and where a particular condition is found. The thematic maps in this atlas give you information about specific topics or themes.

This atlas has ten world thematic maps. These maps let you compare the same kinds of information for areas around the world. For example, you could use the World Climate Map to see what places in the world have a climate similar to the climate where you live.

This atlas also has thematic maps in the sections about each of the continents. Several different thematic maps often appear on the same page. This allows you to compare different topics for the same area. For example, if you compare a climate map and a population density map for Africa, what do you think you might discover?

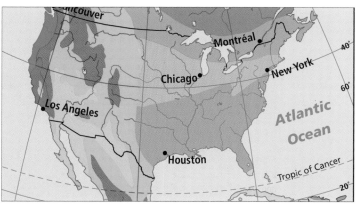

Did you know?

Each "Did You Know?" presents an interesting fact about the world.

Did You Know?

Lake Michigan gets its name from an Algonquin Indian word, *michigami*, which means "big lake."

What If?

Each "What If?" asks you to use information from the atlas and other sources to answer a critical thinking question. There are no right or wrong answers, but be sure you can present facts to support your opinions.

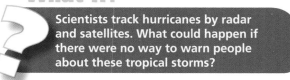

What If?

Scientists track hurricanes by radar and satellites. What could happen if there were no way to warn people about these tropical storms?

Graphs, Charts, and Photographs

The graphs, charts, and photographs in the atlas help illustrate information from the maps. They may help you see the same information in a different way. They may also provide additional information about the themes of the maps. The photographs show you how the features shown on the map look in the real world.

World Export of Oats

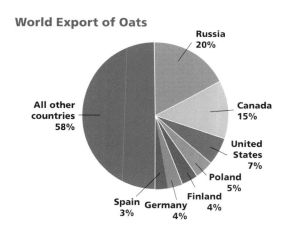

Russia 20%
Canada 15%
United States 7%
Poland 5%
Finland 4%
Germany 4%
Spain 3%
All other countries 58%

Automobiles per 1,000 people

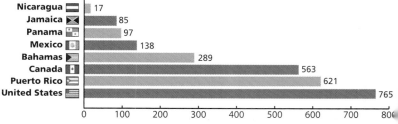

Nicaragua	17
Jamaica	85
Panama	97
Mexico	138
Bahamas	289
Canada	563
Puerto Rico	621
United States	765

0 100 200 300 400 500 600 700 800

Legend for Physical and Political Maps

Water Features

ATLANTIC OCEAN — Ocean or sea

Lake (physical map)

Lake (political map)

Salt lake (physical map)

Salt lake (political map)

Seasonal lake

Nile — River

Niagara Falls — Waterfall

Land Features

ASIA — Continent

Mt. Mitchell 6,684 ft. △ 2,037 m. — Mountain peak

Kilimanjaro 19,340 ft. ▲ 5,895 m. — Highest mountain peak

Alps — Physical feature
(mountain range, desert, plateau, etc.)

Borneo — Island

Cultural Features

———— International boundary

———— State, province, or territory boundary

EGYPT — Country

KANSAS — State, province, or territory

PUERTO RICO (U.S.) — Dependency

Population Centers

National capital	State, province, or territory capital	Town	Population
✪	✸	■	Over 1,000,000
✪	✸	▣	250,000 — 1,000,000
✪	✸	·	Under 250,000

Land Elevations and Ocean Depths

Land elevation

3,000 meters	9,840 feet
2,000 meters	6,560 feet
1,000 meters	3,280 feet
500 meters	1,640 feet
200 meters	656 feet
0 Sea level	0 Sea level

Water depth

0 Sea level	0 Sea level
200 meters	656 feet
2,000 meters	6,560 feet

Geographical Terms

The large illustration to the right is a view of an imaginary place. It shows many of Earth's different types of landforms, bodies of water, and human-made features. The following vocabulary list defines many of the features on the map.

See if you can find an example of each feature on the maps in the atlas.

Archipelago
A group of islands

Canyon
A deep, narrow valley with high, steep sides

Coast
Land along a large lake, a sea, or an ocean

Desert
A large land area that receives very little rainfall

Forest
A large area covered with trees

Gulf
A large part of an ocean or a sea that lies within a curved coastline; A gulf is larger than a bay.

Harbor
A sheltered body of water where ships can safely anchor

Hill
A small area of land that is higher than the land around it

Island
A piece of land that is surrounded by water

Isthmus
A narrow piece of land that joins two larger areas of land

Lake
A body of water completely surrounded by land

Mountain
Land that rises much higher than the land around it

Mountain range
A row of mountains that are joined together

Ocean
One of Earth's largest bodies of water

Plain
A large, flat land area

Plateau
A large area of land where the highest elevation is generally the same; A plateau may have deep valleys.

River
A body of fresh water that flows from higher to lower land; A river usually flows into another river, a lake, a sea, or an ocean.

Sea
A large body of salt water nearly or partly surrounded by land; A sea is much smaller than an ocean.

Valley
Lower land between hills or mountains

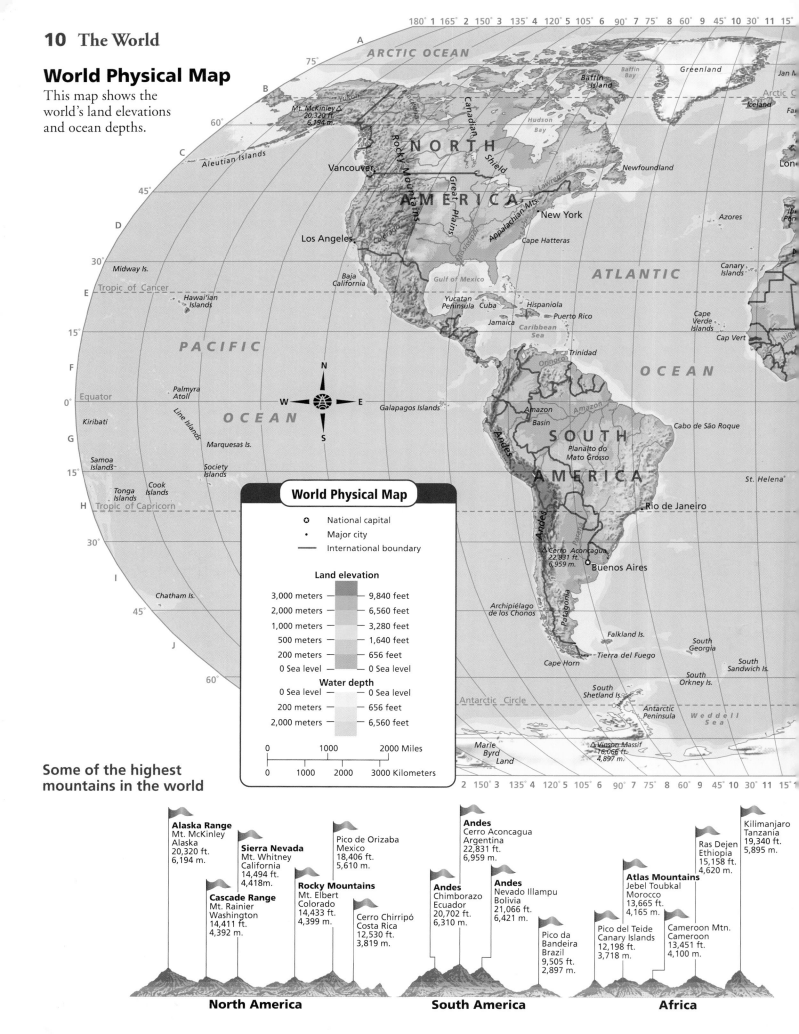

World Physical Map

This map shows the world's land elevations and ocean depths.

World Physical Map

- ⊙ National capital
- • Major city
- — International boundary

Land elevation

3,000 meters	9,840 feet
2,000 meters	6,560 feet
1,000 meters	3,280 feet
500 meters	1,640 feet
200 meters	656 feet
0 Sea level	0 Sea level

Water depth

0 Sea level	0 Sea level
200 meters	656 feet
2,000 meters	6,560 feet

0   1000   2000 Miles
0 1000 2000 3000 Kilometers

Some of the highest mountains in the world

North America

Alaska Range
Mt. McKinley
Alaska
20,320 ft.
6,194 m.

Sierra Nevada
Mt. Whitney
California
14,494 ft.
4,418 m.

Cascade Range
Mt. Rainier
Washington
14,411 ft.
4,392 m.

Rocky Mountains
Mt. Elbert
Colorado
14,433 ft.
4,399 m.

Pico de Orizaba
Mexico
18,406 ft.
5,610 m.

Cerro Chirripó
Costa Rica
12,530 ft.
3,819 m.

South America

Andes
Cerro Aconcagua
Argentina
22,831 ft.
6,959 m.

Andes
Chimborazo
Ecuador
20,702 ft.
6,310 m.

Andes
Nevado Illampu
Bolivia
21,066 ft.
6,421 m.

Pico da
Bandeira
Brazil
9,505 ft.
2,897 m.

Africa

Kilimanjaro
Tanzania
19,340 ft.
5,895 m.

Ras Dejen
Ethiopia
15,158 ft.
4,620 m.

Atlas Mountains
Jebel Toubkal
Morocco
13,665 ft.
4,165 m.

Pico del Teide
Canary Islands
12,198 ft.
3,718 m.

Cameroon Mtn.
Cameroon
13,451 ft.
4,100 m.

World Political Map

People have divided up Earth's land into almost 200 countries. A few of these countries are more than a thousand years old, but most have been formed in the last 200 years.

180° **1** 165° **2** 150° **3** 135° **4** 120° **5** 105° **6** 90° **7** 75° **8** 60° **9** 45° **10** 30° **11** 15°

A

ARCTIC OCEAN

Baffin Bay

GREENLAND
(Denmark)

75°

B

RUSSIA

ALASKA
(U.S.)

Yukon

Hudson Bay

ICELAND

60°

Anchorage

UNITED KINGDOM

C

Aleutian Islands

C A N A D A

Vancouver

Newfoundland

IRELAND

London

45°

Montréal
Ottawa

D

Chicago

U N I T E D   S T A T E S

New York
Washington, D.C.

Azores (Port.)

PORTUGAL

Madrid

30°

MIDWAY IS.
(U.S.)

Los Angeles

Colorado

Houston

Canary Islands (Sp.)

Casablanca

MOROCCO

E

Tropic of Cancer

Hawai'ian Islands (U.S.)

MEXICO

Gulf of Mexico

BAHAMAS

ATLANTIC

W. SAHARA

CAPE VERDE

MAURITANIA

15°

Mexico City

CUBA

HAITI
DOM. REP.

PUERTO RICO (U.S.)

SENEGAL

F

P A C I F I C

BELIZE
GUAT. HOND.
EL SAL. NIC.

JAMAICA

Caribbean Sea

Caracas

TRINIDAD AND TOBAGO

GUINEA-BISSAU

GUINEA

SIERRA LEONE

CÔTE D'IVOIRE

LIBERIA

Equator

COSTA RICA
PANAMA

VENEZUELA GUYANA
SURINAME
FRENCH GUIANA (Fr.)

Niger

0°

KIRIBATI

COLOMBIA

Amazon

ECUADOR

Galapagos Islands (Ecuador)

G

SAMOA

PERU

B R A Z I L

O C E A N

15°

AMERICAN SAMOA
(U.S.)

COOK ISLANDS
(N.Z.)

Lima

TONGA

FRENCH POLYNESIA
(Fr.)

BOLIVIA

Brasília

ST. HELENA (U.K.)

H

Tropic of Capricorn

Easter Island (Chile)

PARAGUAY

Rio de Janeiro

30°

ARGENTINA

I

International Date Line

Santiago

CHILE

URUGUAY

Buenos Aires

45°

World Political Map

⊙ National capital

• Major city

—— International boundary

J

FALKLAND IS.
(U.K.)

South Georgia (U.K.)

0   1000   2000 Miles

0   1000   2000   3000 Kilometers

60°

South Orkney Is. (U.K.)

K

Antarctic Circle

S O U T H E R N   O C E A N

South Shetland Is. (U.K.)

Weddell Sea

75°

L

180° **1** 165° **2** 150° **3** 135° **4** 120° **5** 105° **6** 90° **7** 75° **8** 60° **9** 45° **10** 30° **11** 15°

World Climate Map

This map shows climate conditions throughout the world. Climate is the average **weather conditions** over a long period of time. Temperature and precipitation together make up climate.

Climate Graphs

Each of the climate graphs below shows the average temperature and **precipitation** for every month of the year. Precipitation is rain, snow, sleet, or hail.

The 12 letters below each graph are the first letters of the twelve months, beginning with January (J) and ending with December (D). There is one climate graph for every type of climate region in the world.

Curved lines on the graphs show temperatures in degrees Celsius and degrees Fahrenheit. The numbers are to the left of the graphs.

Vertical bars on the graphs show monthly precipitation in inches and centimeters. The numbers are to the right of the graphs.

Colors on the graphs match colors on the map. The cities for the graphs are also shown on the map.

Climate Map

Tropical
- Hot with rain all year
- Hot with seasonal rain

Dry
- Desert
- Some rain

Moderate (Rainy Winter)
- Hot, dry summer
- Hot, humid summer
- Mild, rainy summer

Continental (Snowy Winter)
- Long, warm, humid summer
- Short, cool, humid summer
- Very short, cool, humid summer

Polar
- Tundra – very cold and dry
- Ice cap

Highlands
- Varies with altitude

© Rand McNally
Made in U.S.A.
M-102168-3

ATLANTIC OCEAN

PACIFIC OCEAN

Barrow
Arctic Circle
Vancouver
Montréal
Chicago
New York
Los Angeles
Houston
Tropic of Cancer
Mexico City
Caracas
Equator
Tropic of Capricorn
Recife
Rio de Janeiro
Buenos Aires
Antarctic Circle

Temperature

Precipitation

°C	°F
38	100
27	80
16	60
4	40
-7	20
-18	0
-29	-20
-40	-40

in.	cm.
14	36
12	30
10	25
8	20
6	15
4	10
2	5
0	0

Jakarta, Indonesia
JFMAMJJASOND
Tropical
Hot with rain all year

Darwin, Australia
JFMAMJJASOND
Tropical
Hot with seasonal rain

Cairo, Egypt
JFMAMJJASOND
Dry
Desert

Tehran, Iran
JFMAMJJASOND
Dry
Some rain

Los Angeles, California, U.S.
JFMAMJJASOND
Moderate
Hot, dry summer

Buenos Aires, Argentina
JFMAMJJASOND
Moderate
Hot, humid summer

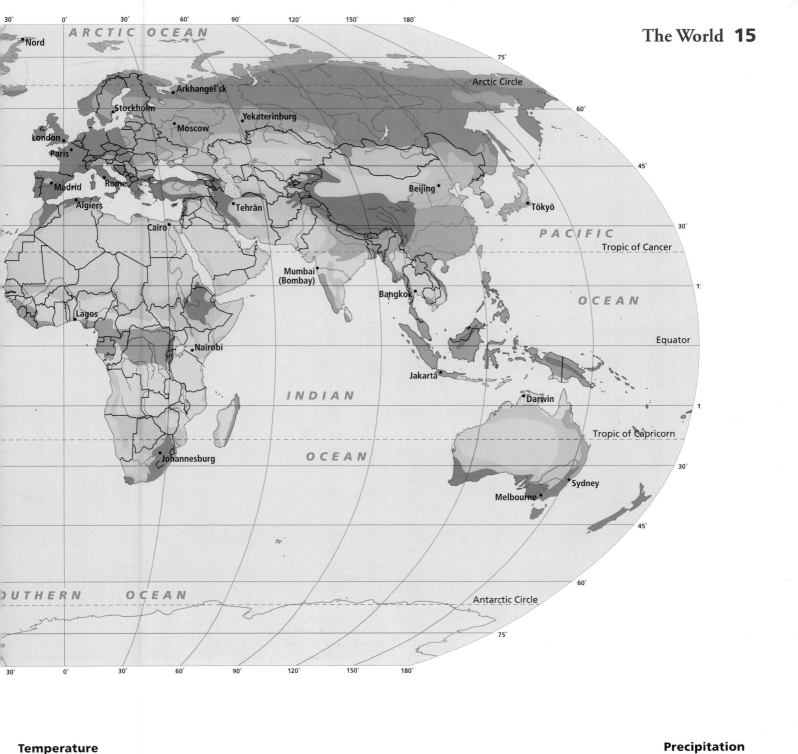

ARCTIC OCEAN

Nord

Arctic Circle

Arkhangel'sk

Stockholm

Moscow

Yekaterinburg

London

Paris

Madrid

Rome

Algiers

Tehrān

Beijing

Tōkyō

PACIFIC

Cairo

Tropic of Cancer

OCEAN

Lagos

Mumbai
(Bombay)

Bangkok

Nairobi

Equator

Jakarta

INDIAN

Darwin

OCEAN

Tropic of Capricorn

Johannesburg

Sydney

Melbourne

SOUTHERN   OCEAN

Antarctic Circle

Temperature

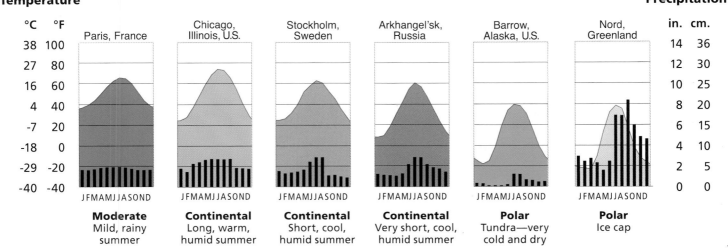

°C	°F	Paris, France	Chicago, Illinois, U.S.	Stockholm, Sweden	Arkhangel'sk, Russia	Barrow, Alaska, U.S.	Nord, Greenland
38	100						
27	80						
16	60						
4	40						
-7	20						
-18	0						
-29	-20						
-40	-40						
		JFMAMJJASOND	JFMAMJJASOND	JFMAMJJASOND	JFMAMJJASOND	JFMAMJJASOND	JFMAMJJASOND

Precipitation

in.	cm.
14	36
12	30
10	25
8	20
6	15
4	10
2	5
0	0

Moderate
Mild, rainy
summer

Continental
Long, warm,
humid summer

Continental
Short, cool,
humid summer

Continental
Very short, cool,
humid summer

Polar
Tundra—very
cold and dry

Polar
Ice cap

World Environments Map

This map shows different environments throughout the world. The environment of a place is its physical setting and conditions. Some environments, such as forest and tundra, are natural. Other environments, such as cropland and urban areas, have been created by humans. This map shows many of the world's largest urban areas.

The theme of this map is land environments, but approximately 75% of Earth's surface is covered by water. This causes Earth to look blue from space. For this reason, Earth is sometimes called the "blue marble."

Only 3% of the water on Earth is fresh water. The other 97% of Earth's water is salt water.

Environments Map

- Forest
- Swamp
- Crop & woodland
- Cropland
- Crop & grazing land
- Grassland
- Desert
- Tundra
- Barren
- Urban

© Rand McNally
Made in U.S.A
M-102169-3

Earth as seen from space

Forest

Swamp

Crop and woodland

Cropland

Crop and grazing land

ARCTIC OCEAN

75°

Arctic Circle

60°

Stockholm

Moscow

45°

London

Paris

Beijing

Tōkyō

Madrid Rome

Tehrān

PACIFIC

30°

Algiers

Cairo

Tropic of Cancer

1

OCEAN

Mumbai
(Bombay)

Bangkok

Lagos

Equator

Nairobi

Jakarta

INDIAN

1

Tropic of Capricorn

Johannesburg

OCEAN

Sydney

30°

Melbourne

45°

OUTHERN   OCEAN

60°

Antarctic Circle

75°

Grassland

Desert

Tundra

Barren

Urban

World Population Density Map

This map shows which parts of the world have many people and which have few people. Areas with many people living there have **dense** populations. The largest areas of dense populations are in East Asia, South Asia, and Europe. Vast areas of the world are too cold, too dry, or too mountainous for dense population.

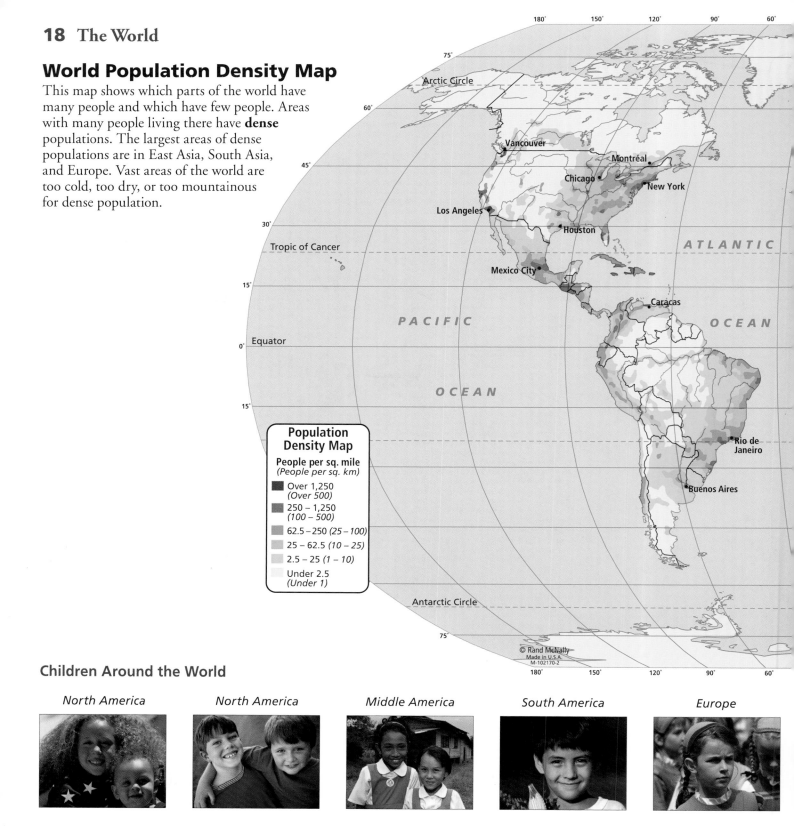

Population Density Map

People per sq. mile
(People per sq. km)

- Over 1,250 *(Over 500)*
- 250 – 1,250 *(100 – 500)*
- 62.5 – 250 *(25 – 100)*
- 25 – 62.5 *(10 – 25)*
- 2.5 – 25 *(1 – 10)*
- Under 2.5 *(Under 1)*

© Rand McNally
Made in U.S.A.
M-102170-2

Children Around the World

North America

North America

Middle America

South America

Europe

World Population Growth

For most of human history, the world's population grew very slowly. About 250 years ago, it began to grow faster as people learned to control illnesses. However, today people in many parts of the world are having smaller families, and the rate of growth may be slowing down.

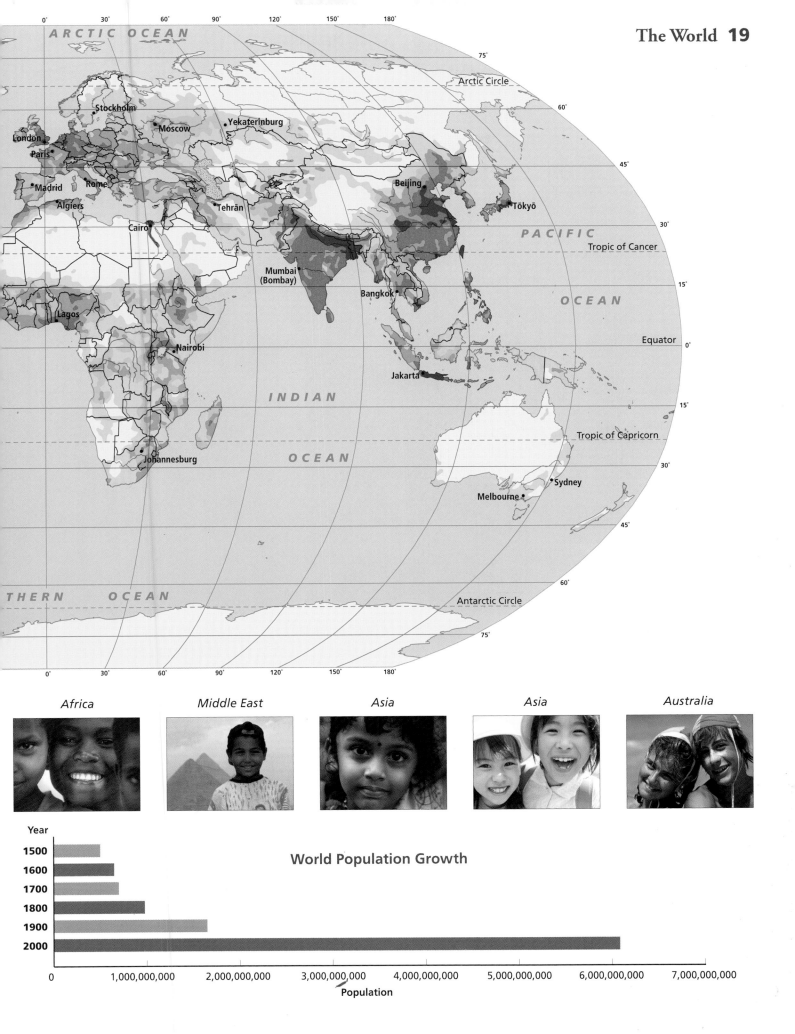

ARCTIC OCEAN

Arctic Circle

PACIFIC

OCEAN

Tropic of Cancer

Equator

INDIAN

OCEAN

Tropic of Capricorn

THERN   OCEAN

Antarctic Circle

Stockholm
Moscow
Yekaterinburg
London
Paris
Madrid
Rome
Algiers
Cairo
Tehrān
Beijing
Tōkyō
Mumbai (Bombay)
Bangkok
Lagos
Nairobi
Jakarta
Johannesburg
Sydney
Melbourne

Africa

Middle East

Asia

Asia

Australia

World Population Growth

Year	
1500	
1600	
1700	
1800	
1900	
2000	

0   1,000,000,000   2,000,000,000   3,000,000,000   4,000,000,000   5,000,000,000   6,000,000,000   7,000,000,000

Population

World Patterns of Economic Activity

This map shows the kinds of jobs people have around the world. Each color on the map shows the most important economic activity for that area.

Look at the bright yellow area of Canada and the United States. According to the map legend, agriculture is the most important economic activity there. If you went to this area, you would see farm fields, orchards, and farm animals such as dairy cows and pigs. You would probably see grain elevators, feed stores, and other businesses that support farming. Of course, you would see banks, office buildings, stores, and factories, but not as many as you would see in the areas colored red.

According to the map legend, the most important economic activities in the red areas are manufacturing and commerce. Manufacturing is making goods. Automobiles, computers, clothing, and skateboards are examples of goods.

Commerce is the buying and selling of goods. Commerce also includes the buying and selling of services. Medical care, banking, education, and cable television are examples of service industries. In Canada, the United States, Europe, and Japan, more people work in service industries than in manufacturing or agriculture. If you went to the areas shown in red, you would see a concentration of banks, office buildings, factories, and stores. Many of the world's largest manufacturing and commerce areas are shown on this map.

According to the map legend, hunting, forestry, and subsistence farming are the most important economic activities in the brown areas. In these areas you would find people working on small farms, growing food for themselves and their families. You would find people hunting and fishing to get food for themselves and their families.

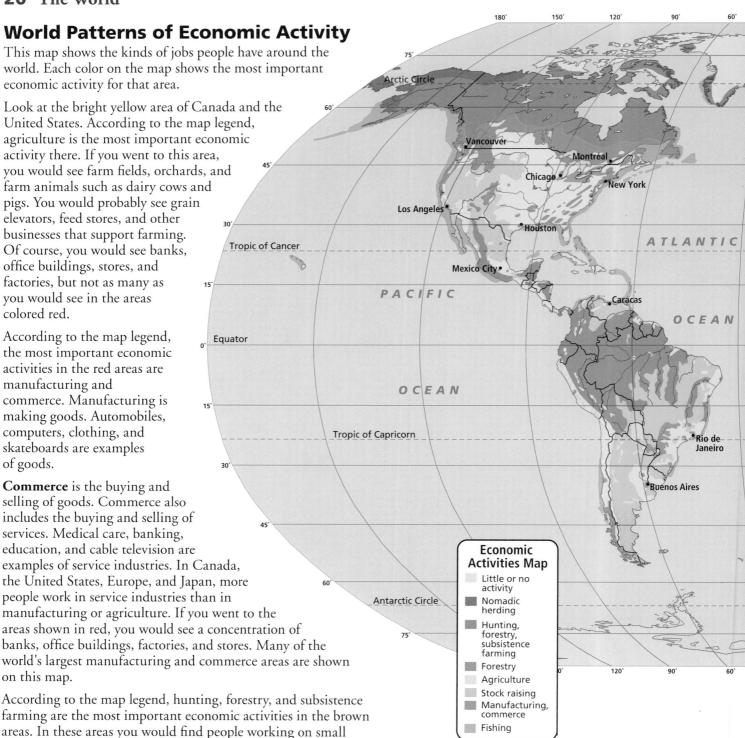

Economic Activities Map

- Little or no activity
- Nomadic herding
- Hunting, forestry, subsistence farming
- Forestry
- Agriculture
- Stock raising
- Manufacturing, commerce
- Fishing

Nomadic herding

Hunting

Subsistence farming

Forestry

Agriculture

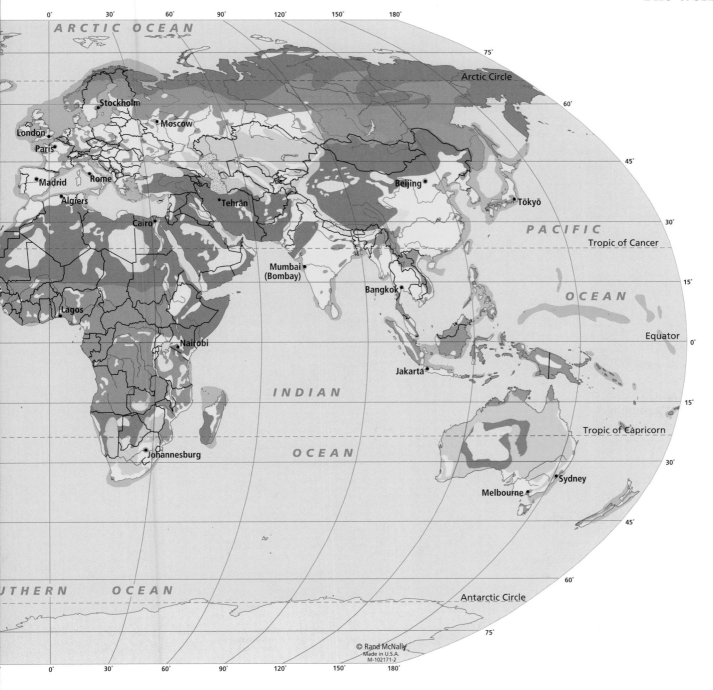

ARCTIC OCEAN

75°

Arctic Circle

60°

Stockholm

Moscow

45°

London

Paris

Madrid • Rome

Beijing

30°

Algiers

Tehrān

Tōkyō

Cairo

PACIFIC

Tropic of Cancer

Mumbai
(Bombay)

15°

Bangkok

OCEAN

Lagos

Nairobi

INDIAN

Equator 0°

Jakarta

15°

OCEAN

Tropic of Capricorn

Johannesburg

30°

Sydney

Melbourne

45°

SOUTHERN   OCEAN

60°

Antarctic Circle

75°

© Rand McNally
Made in U.S.A.
M-102171-2

Agriculture

Stock raising

Manufacturing

Commerce

Fishing

World Mineral Fuel Deposits

Deposits of coal, petroleum, and natural gas are found in very limited parts of the world. What types of deposits does the United States have? Which continents have many coal deposits?

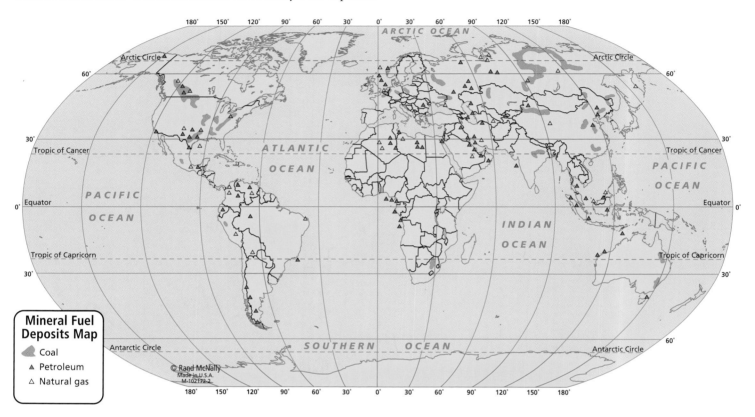

Mineral Fuel Deposits Map

- Coal
- ▲ Petroleum
- △ Natural gas

© Rand McNally
Made in U.S.A.
M-102172-2

World Coal Production

China and the United States, which have extensive deposits of coal, lead the world in coal production.

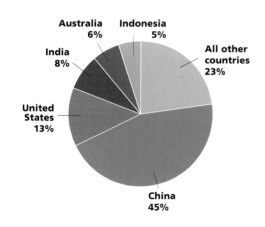

Australia 6%
Indonesia 5%
India 8%
All other countries 23%
United States 13%
China 45%

World Petroleum Production

Saudi Arabia, Russia, and the United States produce more than one-third of the world's oil.

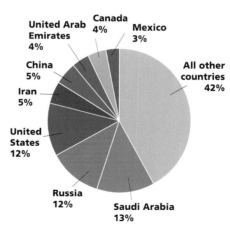

United Arab Emirates 4%
Canada 4%
Mexico 3%
China 5%
All other countries 42%
Iran 5%
United States 12%
Russia 12%
Saudi Arabia 13%

World Uranium Production

Australia and Kazakhstan lead the world in production of uranium, which is used as a fuel in nuclear energy plants.

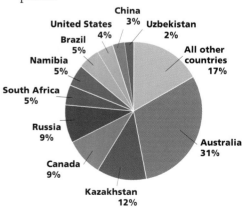

China 3%
United States 4%
Uzbekistan 2%
Brazil 5%
Namibia 5%
All other countries 17%
South Africa 5%
Russia 9%
Australia 31%
Canada 9%
Kazakhstan 12%

World Energy Consumption

Manufacturing, heating, and transportation are the three main ways that people use energy. This explains why the largest users of energy are industrialized countries that have large populations and relatively cold climates.

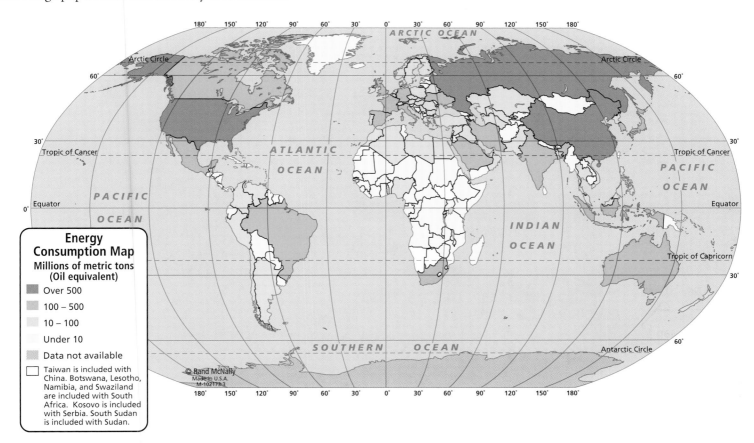

Energy Consumption Map
Millions of metric tons (Oil equivalent)

- Over 500
- 100 – 500
- 10 – 100
- Under 10
- Data not available
- Taiwan is included with China. Botswana, Lesotho, Namibia, and Swaziland are included with South Africa. Kosovo is included with Serbia. South Sudan is included with Sudan.

© Rand McNally
Made in U.S.A.
M-102175-3

Energy Terms

Coal

A rock created from ancient plant life under enormous pressure. It is burned to produce heat and create steam for running machines or making electricity. Most coal, when burned, emits sulfur, a major component of acid rain.

Geothermal power

Uses water heated naturally beneath the earth's surface. The steam that results powers engines that create electricity. Geothermal power is a clean source of energy, but it is available only in very limited areas.

Fossil fuels

Formed from remains of plants and animals over millions of years. Fossil fuels are not renewable sources of energy because it takes vast amounts of time to create them. Coal, oil, and natural gas are fossil fuels.

Hydroelectricity

Generated by fast-moving water that is used to power generators. Dams on rivers provide sources of rapidly moving water. Hydroelectricity is a clean source of power, but the dams can have negative effects on their surroundings.

Natural gas

A form of petroleum, this flammable gas is used mainly as fuel for stoves, furnaces, and hot-water heaters. Natural gas is a clean-burning fuel.

Nuclear energy

Created by splitting atoms. The energy is used to heat water that makes steam to drive electricity generators. The safety of nuclear plants and the hazardous wastes they create are of great concern.

Petroleum

A liquid, also called oil. Petroleum is the most widely used source of energy in the world. It is used to produce gasoline, kerosene, and fuel oil. It is also used to manufacture plastics and other products.

Wind power and solar energy

Two sources of renewable energy. They are not in wide use today, but in some places the use of wind to make electricity is increasing.

Plate Tectonics

According to the theory of plate tectonics, Earth's surface is divided into more than a dozen plates. These plates move very slowly—just a few inches a year. As they move, they collide or grind past each other. Most of the world's volcanoes and earthquakes occur at the places where plates meet.

Many plates collide with or grind past the Pacific Plate. Find the Pacific Plate on the Plate Tectonics map. The Ring of Fire is the name given to the band of earthquakes and volcanic activity around the Pacific Ocean.

225 million years ago: *Most of the world's land was together in a single "supercontinent." Scientists call this giant continent Pangaea.*

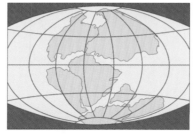

180 million years ago: *Pangaea split up into separate landmasses.*

65 million years ago: *The oceans as we know them today began to take shape. South America and India moved away from Africa.*

The present day: *India has joined with Asia, Australia has moved away from Antarctica, and North America has separated from Europe.*

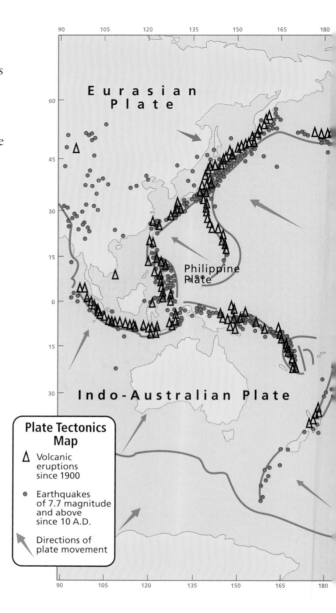

Plate Tectonics Map

Δ Volcanic eruptions since 1900

● Earthquakes of 7.7 magnitude and above since 10 A.D.

↖ Directions of plate movement

Some Notable Earthquakes

Year	Magnitude (Richter Scale)	Place	Estimated Deaths
2011	9.0	Near Honshū, Japan	20,352
2010	7.0	Near Port-au-Prince, Haiti	316,000
2004	9.1	Sumatra, Indonesia	227,000 killed by earthquake and tsunami
1990	7.4	Iran	50,000 killed by earthquake and landslides
1976	7.5	Tangshan, China	255,000
1970	7.9	Peru	66,000
1964	9.2	Prince William Sound, AK	128 killed by earthquake and tsunami
1948	7.3	Turkmenistan	110,000
1927	7.9	Qinghai, China	200,000
1923	7.9	Japan	143,000 killed by earthquake and fire
1908	7.2	Italy	70,000 killed by earthquake and tsunami
1906	7.8	San Francisco, CA	3,000 killed by earthquake and fire

Damage from the 1906 San Francisco earthquake

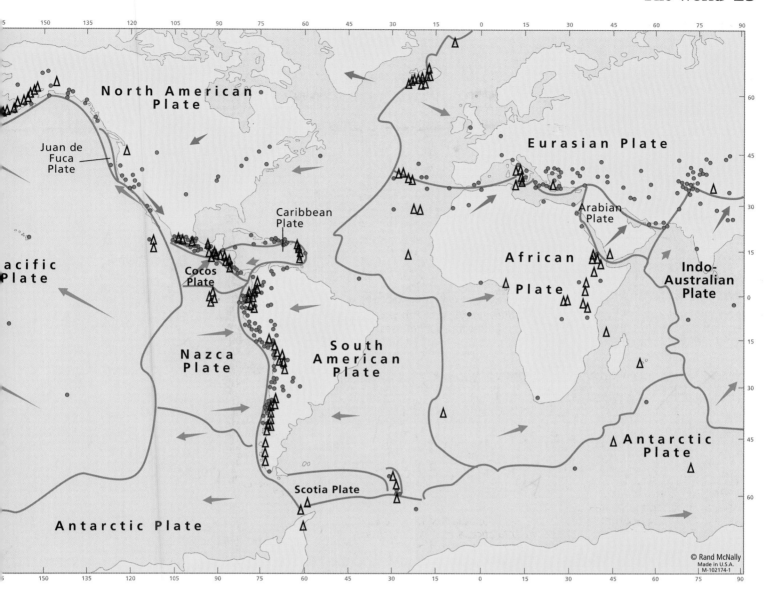

Some Notable Volcanic Eruptions

Year	Volcanic Explosivity Index (VEI)	Name (location)	Estimated Deaths
2010	4	Eyjafjallajökull (Iceland)	Disrupted air travel for 20 countries
1991	6	Mt. Pinatubo (Philippines)	900
1985	3	Nevado del Ruiz (Colombia)	25,000
1980	5	Mt. St. Helens (Washington, U.S.)	57
1963	3	Surtsey (Iceland)	Volcano creates new island
1902	4	Mt. Pelée (Martinique)	30,000
1883	6	Krakatoa (Indonesia)	36,000 killed, most by tsunami
1815	7	Gunung Tambora (Indonesia)	92,000
79	5	Vesuvius (Italy)	16,000 killed in Pompeii and Herculaneum

Eruption of Mt. St. Helens in 1980

World Time Zones

The world is divided into 24 standard time zones. As Earth turns on its axis each day, the sun is overhead at different places at different times. Each time zone is based on the place where the sun is overhead at noon. The boundaries are adjusted so that people whose activities are connected live in the same time zone.

You can figure out the standard time for any time zone in the world. Add one hour for each time you count as you go east. Subtract one hour for each time zone you count as you go west.

Prime Meridian

The Prime Meridian is also called the Greenwich Meridian because it is centered on the Royal Greenwich Observatory near London in the United Kingdom. It represents 0° longitude. Time around the world is counted from the Prime Meridian.

International Date Line

The International Date Line is halfway around the world from the Prime Meridian, at 180° longitude. Like time zone boundaries, the International Date Line is adjusted from 180° so that people in the same country have the same day. The time is the same on both sides of the International Date Line, but the day is different. West of the International Date Line it is one day later than it is east of the International Date Line.

New Zealand, which lies just west of the International Date Line, is one of the first places in the world to greet each new day.

The precise location of the Prime Meridian is marked at the Royal Greenwich Observatory near London.

Examples of Time Changes

Auckland, New Zealand

12 midnight
June 26

Los Angeles, California, United States

4 a.m.
June 25

Montréal, Québec, Canada

7 a.m.
June 25

Rio de Janeiro, Brazil

9 a.m.
June 25

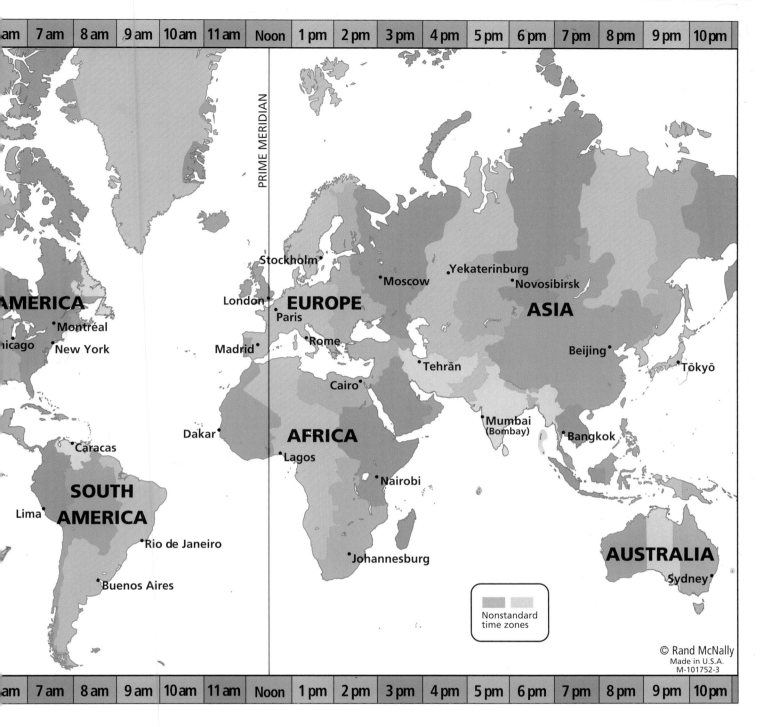

7am	8am	9am	10am	11am	Noon	1pm	2pm	3pm	4pm	5pm	6pm	7pm	8pm	9pm	10pm

PRIME MERIDIAN

Stockholm

Moscow · Yekaterinburg · Novosibirsk

London EUROPE ASIA

Paris

AMERICA Montréal · Rome Beijing · Tōkyō

hicago New York Madrid

Tehrān

Cairo

Dakar AFRICA Mumbai (Bombay) · Bangkok

Caracas Lagos

Nairobi

SOUTH AMERICA

Lima

Rio de Janeiro AUSTRALIA

Johannesburg Sydney

Buenos Aires

Nonstandard time zones

© Rand McNally
Made in U.S.A.
M-101752-3

7am	8am	9am	10am	11am	Noon	1pm	2pm	3pm	4pm	5pm	6pm	7pm	8pm	9pm	10pm

Paris, France

1 p.m.
June 25

Moscow, Russia

3 p.m.
June 25

Novosibirsk, Russia

6 p.m.
June 25

Tōkyō, Japan

9 p.m.
June 25

North America

North America is the third-largest continent. About 506,000,000 people live there.

It stretches more than 5,400 miles (8,700 kilometers) from northern Canada to the Panama-Colombia border.

Three countries—Canada, the United States, and Mexico—make up most of North America. The Caribbean island countries, the countries of Central America, and the island of Greenland make up the rest of the continent.

Central America is a region within North America. It is made up of the countries of Belize, Guatemala, Honduras, El Salvador, Nicaragua, Costa Rica, and Panama.

Central America is part of a larger region of North America called Middle America. This region consists of Central America, Mexico, and the Caribbean countries.

Generally, the people of North America have used its rich natural resources to great advantage. But not everyone has benefited. There are people throughout the continent who struggle with poverty, particularly in Central America and some Caribbean countries.

Mt. McKinley, Alaska, United States

Parliament Hill, Ottawa, Ontario, Canada

San Francisco, California, United States

Pyramid of the Sun, Mexico

Did You Know?

Greenland, which is part of North America, is the largest island in the world.

A Historical Look At North America

About 20,000 years ago
First inhabitants of North America may have arrived from Asia across a land bridge that has since disappeared.

About 5000 B.C.E.
Corn (maize) is first cultivated in Middle America.

About 1200–1500 A.D.
Aztec civilization is dominant in Mexico.

About 1500
Europeans explore North America.

Urbanization in North America

In the late nineteenth century and early twentieth century, many new factories were built in the United States and Canada. People moved from farms to cities to take jobs in factories and offices. They were joined by immigrants from many countries. After World War II, many people in cities moved to suburbs, and urbanized areas began to grow, especially along the East Coast between Boston and Washington, D.C. Today, people in Mexico are moving to cities and to suburbs. Some of them cannot find steady jobs, and the cities have trouble providing water, sewers, and schools for the rapidly growing populations.

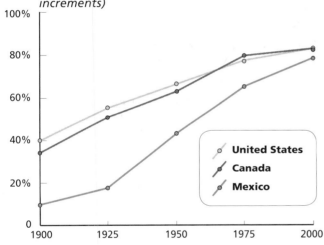

Rising Urban Population
Urban population as a percentage of total population, 1900-2000 (shown in 25-year increments)

- United States
- Canada
- Mexico

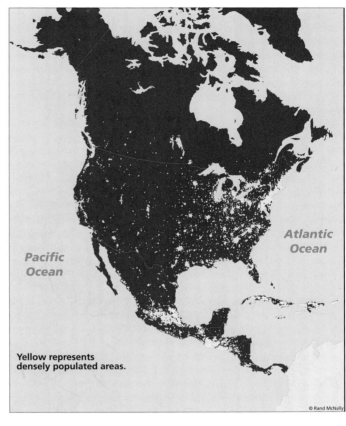

Pacific Ocean

Atlantic Ocean

Yellow represents densely populated areas.

© Rand McNally

New York City, the largest city in the United States

An abandoned farm on the Great Plains

Zachatecas, a city in Mexico

Suburban sprawl in Colorado

Toronto, the largest city in Canada

1776 The United States declares independence.

Mexico becomes independent. **1821**

1867 Canada forms a confederation of four provinces.

1994 Canada, the United States, and Mexico sign the North American Free Trade Agreement, creating the largest free trade area.

The United States celebrates its 200th birthday. **1976**

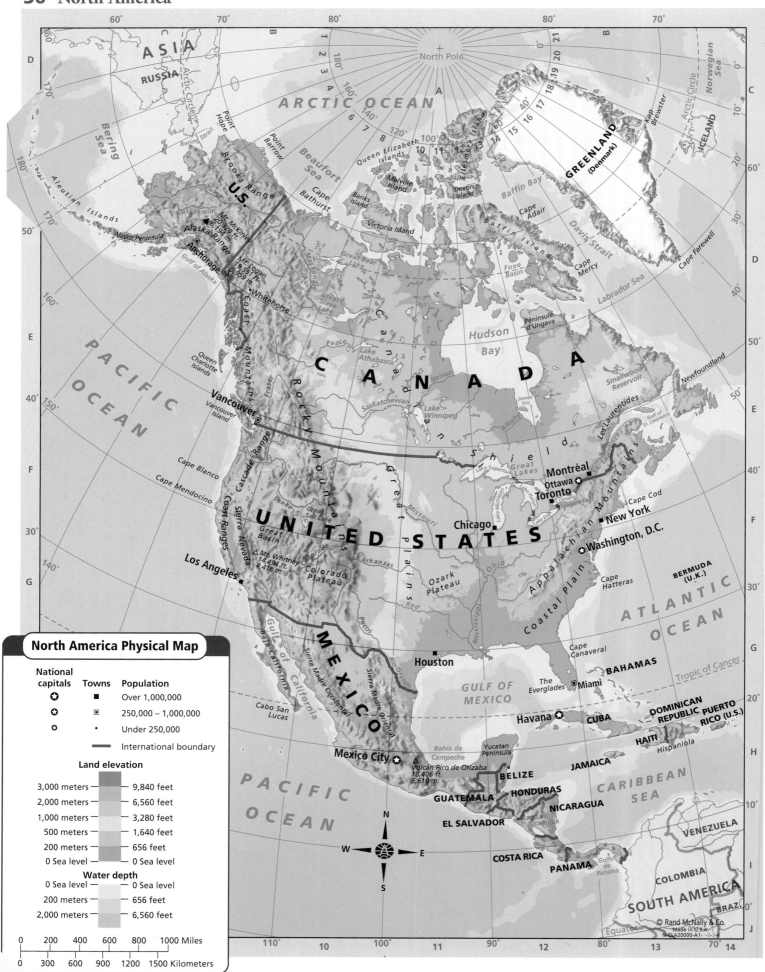

North America Physical Map

National capitals
- ✪ Over 1,000,000
- ✪ 250,000 – 1,000,000
- ✪ Under 250,000

Towns **Population**
- ■ Over 1,000,000
- ▣ 250,000 – 1,000,000
- • Under 250,000

— International boundary

Land elevation

3,000 meters	9,840 feet
2,000 meters	6,560 feet
1,000 meters	3,280 feet
500 meters	1,640 feet
200 meters	656 feet
0 Sea level	0 Sea level

Water depth

0 Sea level	0 Sea level
200 meters	656 feet
2,000 meters	6,560 feet

0 200 400 600 800 1000 Miles

0 300 600 900 1200 1500 Kilometers

© Rand McNally & Co.
Made in U.S.A.
N-CLA20000-A1- -3-14

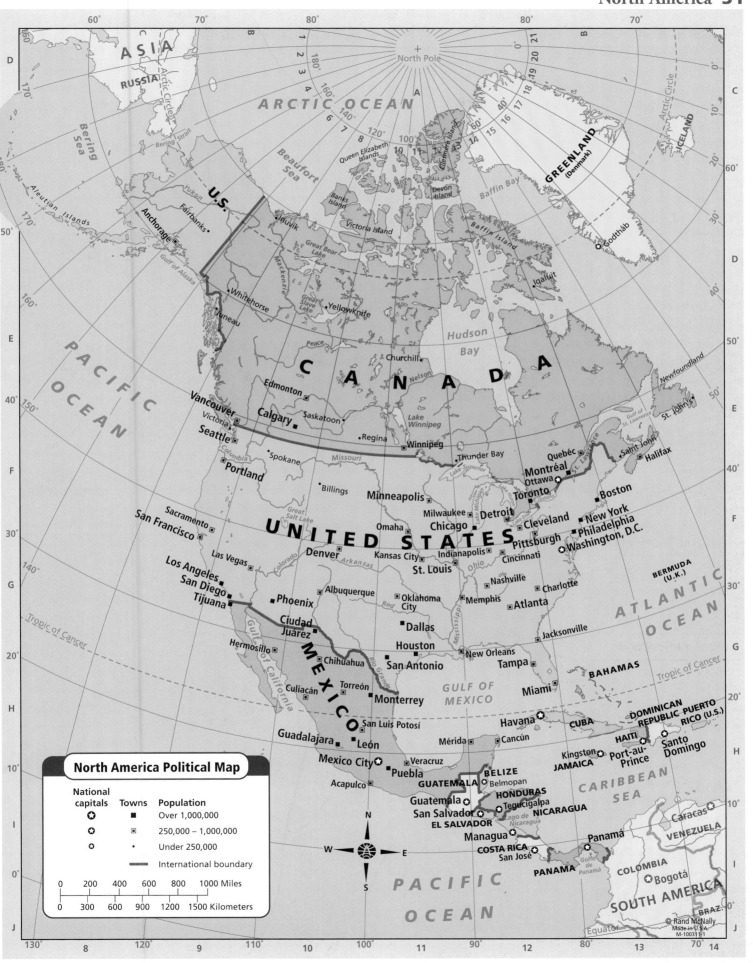

North America Political Map

National capitals	Towns	Population
✪	■	Over 1,000,000
✪	▣	250,000 – 1,000,000
✪	•	Under 250,000
━━		International boundary

0 200 400 600 800 1000 Miles
0 300 600 900 1200 1500 Kilometers

© Rand McNally
Made in U.S.A
M-100311-1

Climate

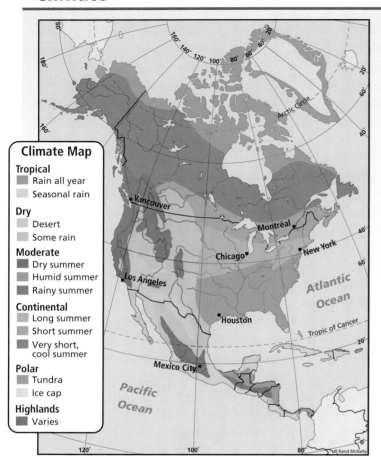

Climate Map

Tropical
- Rain all year
- Seasonal rain

Dry
- Desert
- Some rain

Moderate
- Dry summer
- Humid summer
- Rainy summer

Continental
- Long summer
- Short summer
- Very short, cool summer

Polar
- Tundra
- Ice cap

Highlands
- Varies

Vancouver • Montréal • Chicago • New York • Los Angeles • Houston • Mexico City

Atlantic Ocean · Pacific Ocean · Arctic Circle · Tropic of Cancer

© Rand McNally

Environments

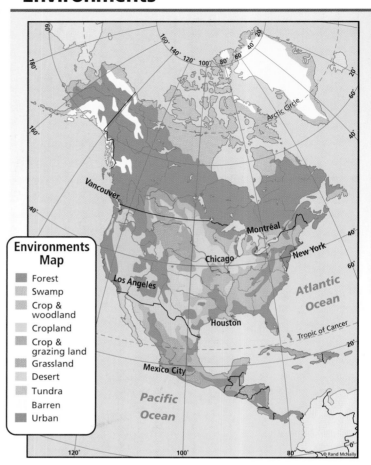

Environments Map
- Forest
- Swamp
- Crop & woodland
- Cropland
- Crop & grazing land
- Grassland
- Desert
- Tundra
- Barren
- Urban

Vancouver • Montréal • Chicago • New York • Los Angeles • Houston • Mexico City

Atlantic Ocean · Pacific Ocean · Arctic Circle · Tropic of Cancer

© Rand McNally

Population

More than one-half of North Americans live in the United States. Canada is the continent's largest country in area, but it is home to only six percent of the continent's population.

North America's Population

- All other countries 15%
- Canada 6%
- Mexico 21%
- United States 58%

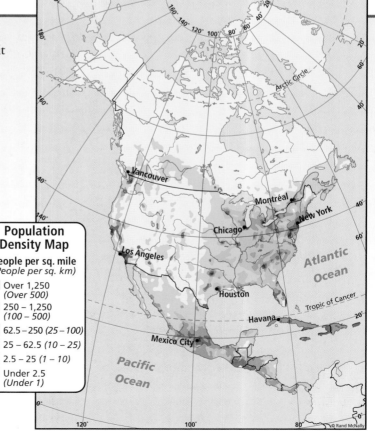

Population Density Map

People per sq. mile
(People per sq. km)
- Over 1,250 *(Over 500)*
- 250 – 1,250 *(100 – 500)*
- 62.5 – 250 *(25 – 100)*
- 25 – 62.5 *(10 – 25)*
- 2.5 – 25 *(1 – 10)*
- Under 2.5 *(Under 1)*

Vancouver • Montréal • Chicago • New York • Los Angeles • Houston • Havana • Mexico City

Atlantic Ocean · Pacific Ocean · Arctic Circle · Tropic of Cancer

© Rand McNally

Vancouver, British Columbia, Canada

Street scene in Chicago, Illinois

Girl in Haiti

The Great Lakes

The Great Lakes lie along the border between the United States and Canada. Canals and rivers allow ocean-going ships to travel to the lakes and between them. Together, the lakes, canals, and rivers form a huge waterway that connects cities far inland with the ocean.

Size rank	Lake	Area sq. miles/ sq. kilometers	Greatest depth feet / meters
1	Superior	31,700 / 82,100	1,332 / 406
2	Huron	23,000 / 59,570	750 / 229
3	Michigan	22,300 / 57,757	925 / 282
4	Erie	9,910 / 25,667	210 / 64
5	Ontario	7,320 / 18,960	802 / 244

Lake Superior is the largest of the Great Lakes.

The Welland Canal in Ontario, Canada, connects Lake Erie and Lake Ontario.

Did You Know?

Lake Michigan gets its name from an Algonquin Indian word, *michigami*, which means "big lake."

Relative Depths of the Great Lakes

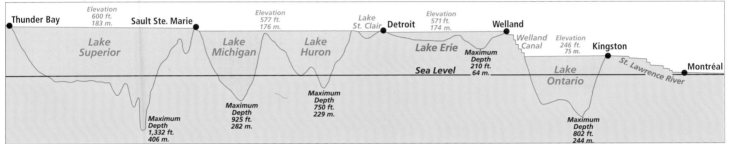

Thunder Bay — Lake Superior — Maximum Depth 1,332 ft. 406 m.

Elevation 600 ft. 183 m.

Sault Ste. Marie

Lake Michigan — Maximum Depth 925 ft. 282 m.

Elevation 577 ft. 176 m.

Lake Huron — Maximum Depth 750 ft. 229 m.

Lake St. Clair — Detroit

Elevation 571 ft. 174 m.

Lake Erie — Maximum Depth 210 ft. 64 m. — Sea Level

Welland — Welland Canal — Elevation 246 ft. 75 m. — Kingston

Lake Ontario — Maximum Depth 802 ft. 244 m.

St. Lawrence River — Montréal

Economic Activities

The map at right shows that agriculture is the most important economic activity for a large part of North America. Much of the continent's manufacturing and commerce is concentrated in a wide band between Chicago and New York.

In 1994, Canada, the United States, and Mexico enacted the North American Free Trade Agreement (NAFTA) to remove all trade restrictions between the three countries.

Fishing trawlers in California

Grain elevators in Alberta, Canada

Factory in Mexico

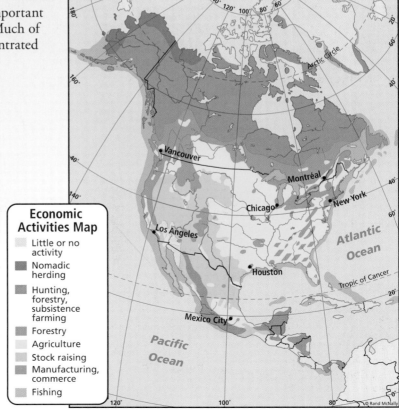

Economic Activities Map

- Little or no activity
- Nomadic herding
- Hunting, forestry, subsistence farming
- Forestry
- Agriculture
- Stock raising
- Manufacturing, commerce
- Fishing

Vancouver, Montréal, Chicago, New York, Los Angeles, Houston, Mexico City

Atlantic Ocean, Pacific Ocean, Arctic Circle, Tropic of Cancer

© Rand McNally

Natural Hazards

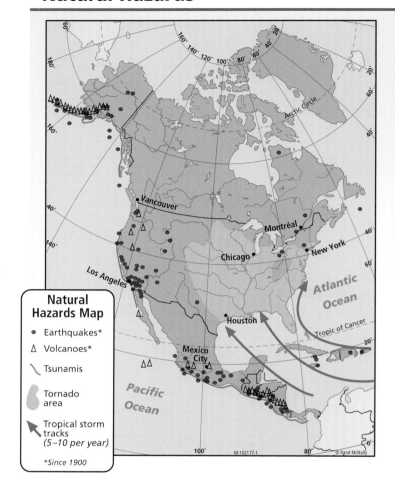

Natural Hazards Map
- Earthquakes*
- △ Volcanoes*
- \ Tsunamis
- Tornado area
- ↖ Tropical storm tracks (5–10 per year)

*Since 1900

This satellite image shows a hurricane approaching the Atlantic coast of Florida.

Twister!

Tornadoes are rapidly rotating columns of air. They are usually funnel-shaped, and their winds may reach 200–500 miles per hour (320–800 kilometers per hour). They are usually less than one-quarter mile (400 meters) wide, but they can be extremely destructive. Texas has more tornadoes than any other state. Oklahoma ranks second in number of tornadoes, and Kansas ranks third.

What If?

Scientists track hurricanes by radar and satellites. What could happen if there were no way to warn people about these tropical storms?

Transportation

Automobiles in Mexico City add to the severe pollution problem there.

Automobiles per 1,000 people
More people in wealthy countries—especially those countries that do not offer much public transportation—own cars.

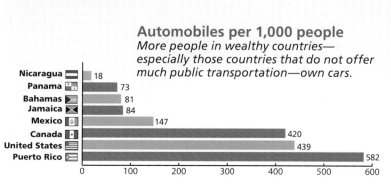

Country	Automobiles per 1,000
Nicaragua	18
Panama	73
Bahamas	81
Jamaica	84
Mexico	147
Canada	420
United States	439
Puerto Rico	582

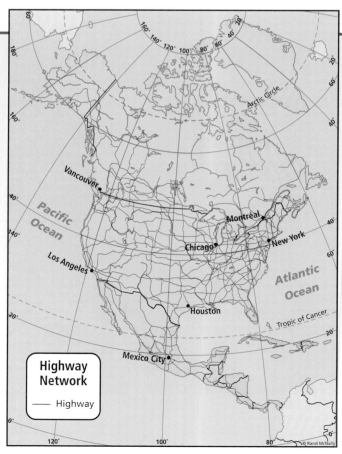

Highway Network
— Highway

Energy

Most nuclear power plants in North America are in the eastern and central United States.

The Hoover Dam in Nevada provides hydroelectric power to three states.

Wind power is a promising alternative energy source.

Electricity Production by Type

More than two-thirds of North America's electricity is produced by power plants that burn coal, oil, and natural gas. This is called thermal energy. Most of the remaining electricity comes from nuclear plants and hydroelectric, or waterpower, plants. Less than one percent of the continent's electricity is produced by geothermal plants, which tap into the heat of Earth's molten interior.

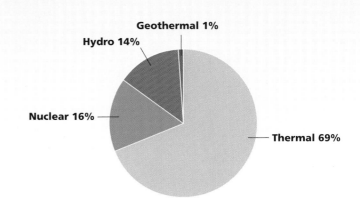

Geothermal 1%
Hydro 14%
Nuclear 16%
Thermal 69%

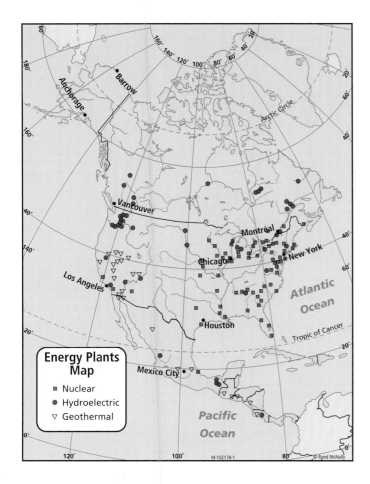

Energy Plants Map

- ■ Nuclear
- ● Hydroelectric
- ▽ Geothermal

M-102178-1 © Rand McNally

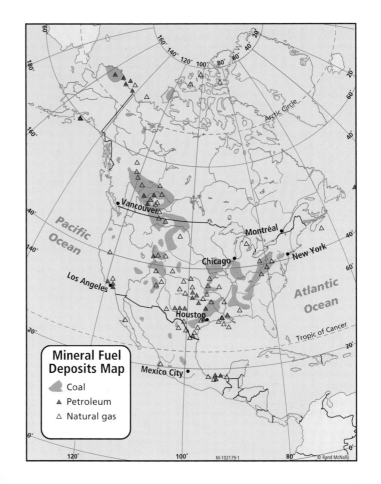

Mineral Fuel Deposits Map

- Coal
- ▲ Petroleum
- △ Natural gas

M-102179-1 © Rand McNally

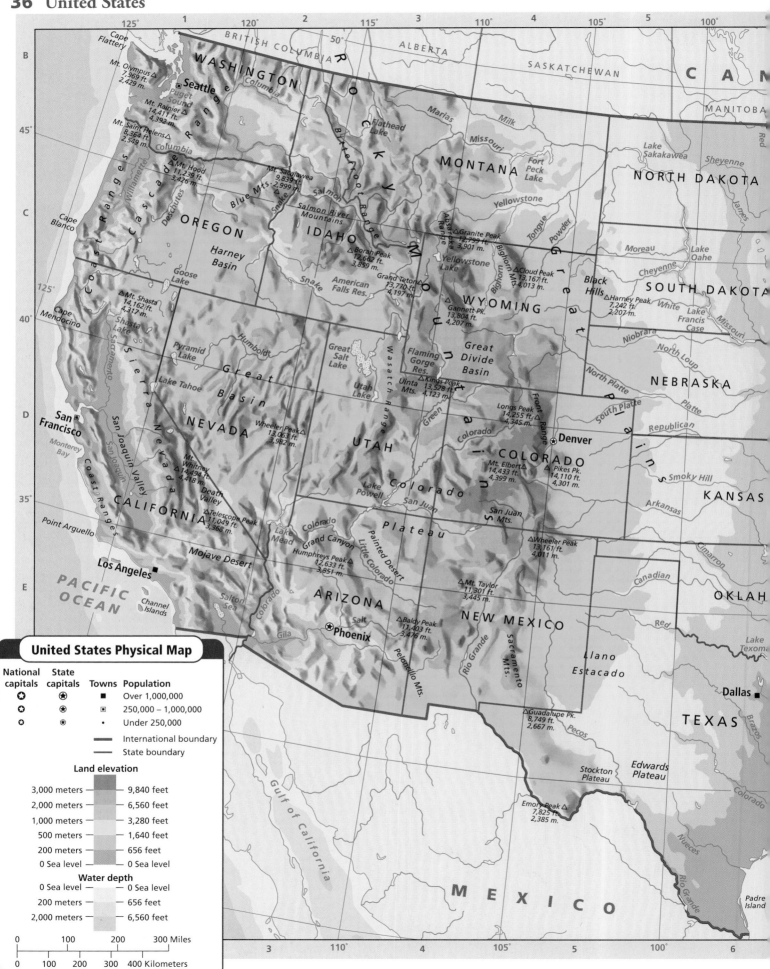

United States Physical Map

National capitals	State capitals	Towns	Population
✪	✪	■	Over 1,000,000
✪	✪	◪	250,000 – 1,000,000
✪	✪	•	Under 250,000
		——	International boundary
		——	State boundary

Land elevation

3,000 meters	9,840 feet
2,000 meters	6,560 feet
1,000 meters	3,280 feet
500 meters	1,640 feet
200 meters	656 feet
0 Sea level	0 Sea level

Water depth

0 Sea level	0 Sea level
200 meters	656 feet
2,000 meters	6,560 feet

0	100	200	300 Miles
0	100	200	300	400 Kilometers

CANADA

ONTARIO

Lake
Winnipeg

Lake
Nipigon

Lake of
the Woods

Isle Royale

Lake Superior

Keweenaw
Peninsula

Whitefish
Point

Great
Lakes

QUÉBEC

St. Lawrence

Ottawa

NEW
BRUNSWICK

Mt. Katahdin
5,268 ft.
△1,606 m.

MAINE

Moosehead
Lake

MINNESOTA

Minneapolis

Minnesota

WISCONSIN

Chippewa

Lake
Winnebago

Wisconsin

Upper Peninsula

MICHIGAN

Green Bay

Muskegon

Lake Michigan

Lower Peninsula

Grand

Saginaw Bay

Lake Huron

Georgian
Bay

Montréal

Ottawa

Lake
Champlain

VERMONT

White
Mts.

Mt. Washington
6,288 ft.
1,917 m.

Adirondack
Mountains

NEW
HAMPSHIRE

Green Mts.

Gulf of
Maine

Toronto

Lake Ontario

Niagara
Falls

NEW YORK

Catskill
Mts.

MASS.   Boston

Cape Cod

IOWA

Iowa

Des Moines

Detroit

Lake Erie

Chicago

Cleveland

Wabash

OHIO

INDIANA

Allegheny Plateau

PENNSYLVANIA

Hudson

CONN.   R.I.

Martha's
Vineyard

Nantucket
Island

New York

Long Island

ILLINOIS

Illinois

White

Mississippi

Scioto

Ohio

Allegheny Mountains

Philadelphia

NEW JERSEY

MISSOURI

Lake of
the Ozarks

St. Louis

Missouri

Green

Lake
Barkley

Lake
Cumberland

Cumberland

WEST
VIRGINIA

Washington, D.C.

Potomac

James

DELAWARE

MARYLAND

Delaware Bay

Chesapeake Bay

Ozark Plateau

Boston
Mts.

White

Neosho

Kentucky Lake

KENTUCKY

TENNESSEE

Cumberland
Plateau

Appalachian

Blue Ridge

Mt. Mitchell
△6,684 ft.
2,037 m.

VIRGINIA

Roanoke

NORTH
CAROLINA

Piedmont

Albemarle
Sound

Pamlico Sound

Cape Hatteras

Cape Lookout

ATLANTIC
OCEAN

ARKANSAS

Ouachita Mts.

Ouachita

Tennessee

Yazoo

Tombigbee

Piedmont

SOUTH
CAROLINA

Santee

Coastal Plain

Cape Fear

Cape Fear

MISSISSIPPI

Mississippi

Pearl

Alabama

ALABAMA

Atlanta

Chattahoochee

Flint

GEORGIA

Savannah

Altamaha

Sea Islands

Sabine

Sam
Rayburn
Res.

Toledo
Bend
Res.

Red

Trinity

LOUISIANA

Lake
Pontchartrain

New
Orleans

Cape
San Blas

Apalachee
Bay

J. Strom
Thurmond
Reservoir

N
W   E
S

Houston

Atchafalaya
Bay

Mississippi
Delta

Suwannee

FLORIDA

Cape Canaveral

GULF OF MEXICO

Tampa Bay

Lake
Okeechobee

The
Everglades

Miami

BAHAMAS

Cape Sable

Florida Keys

B

C

D

A

E

F

G

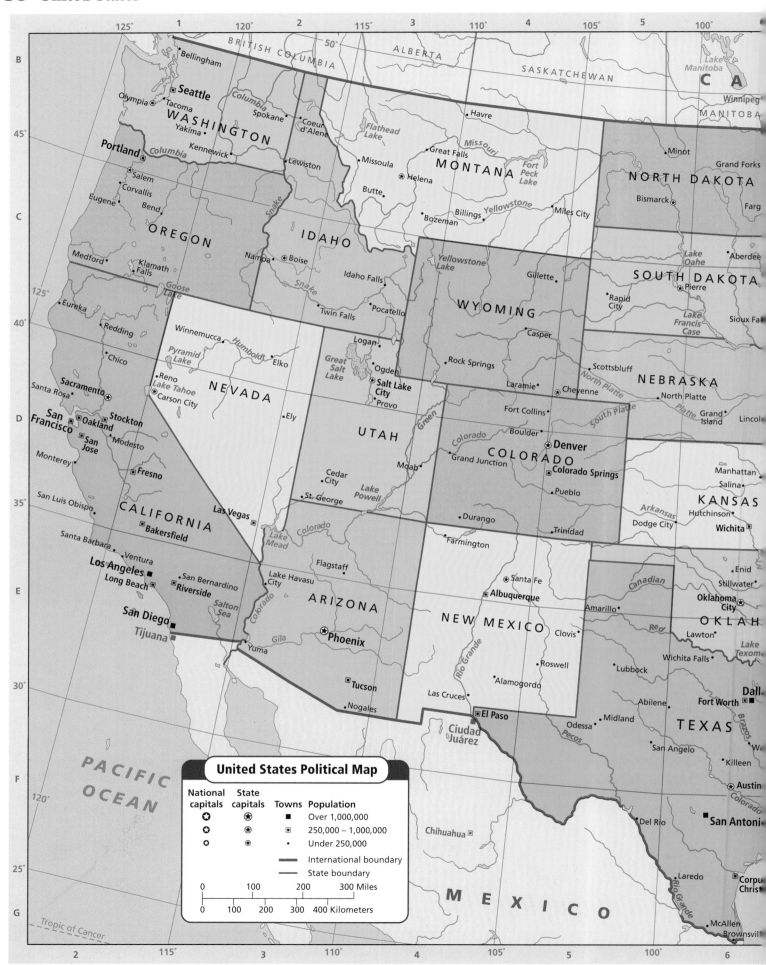

United States Political Map

National capitals	State capitals	Towns	Population
✪	✪	■	Over 1,000,000
✪	✪	▣	250,000 – 1,000,000
✪	✪	•	Under 250,000

━━━ International boundary
─── State boundary

0   100   200   300 Miles
0 100 200 300 400 Kilometers

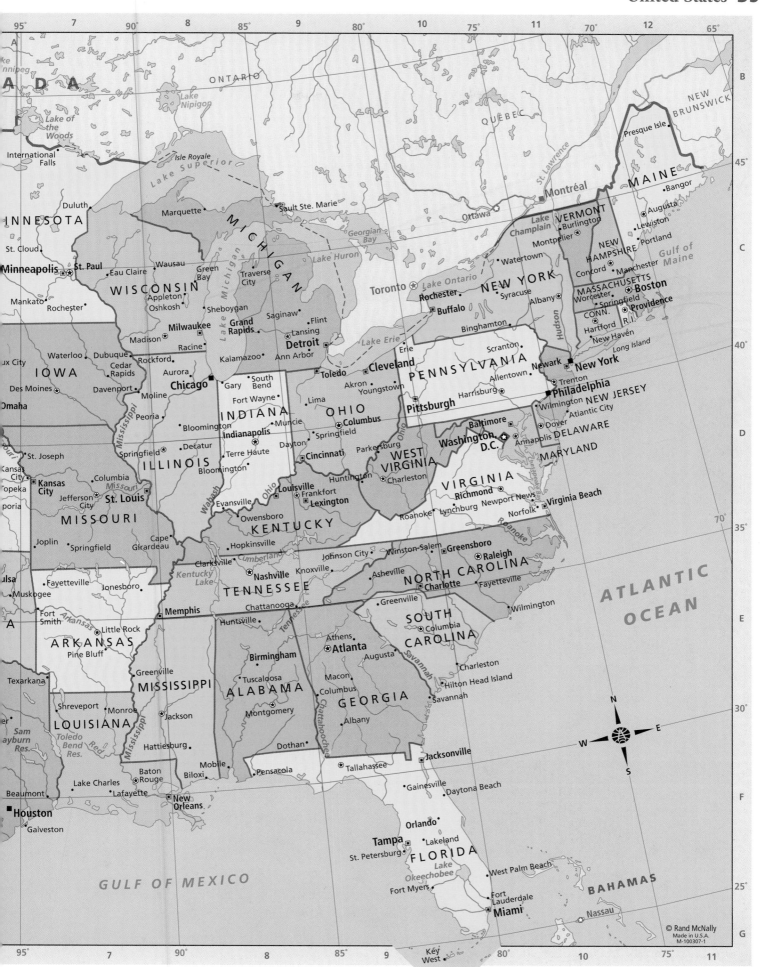

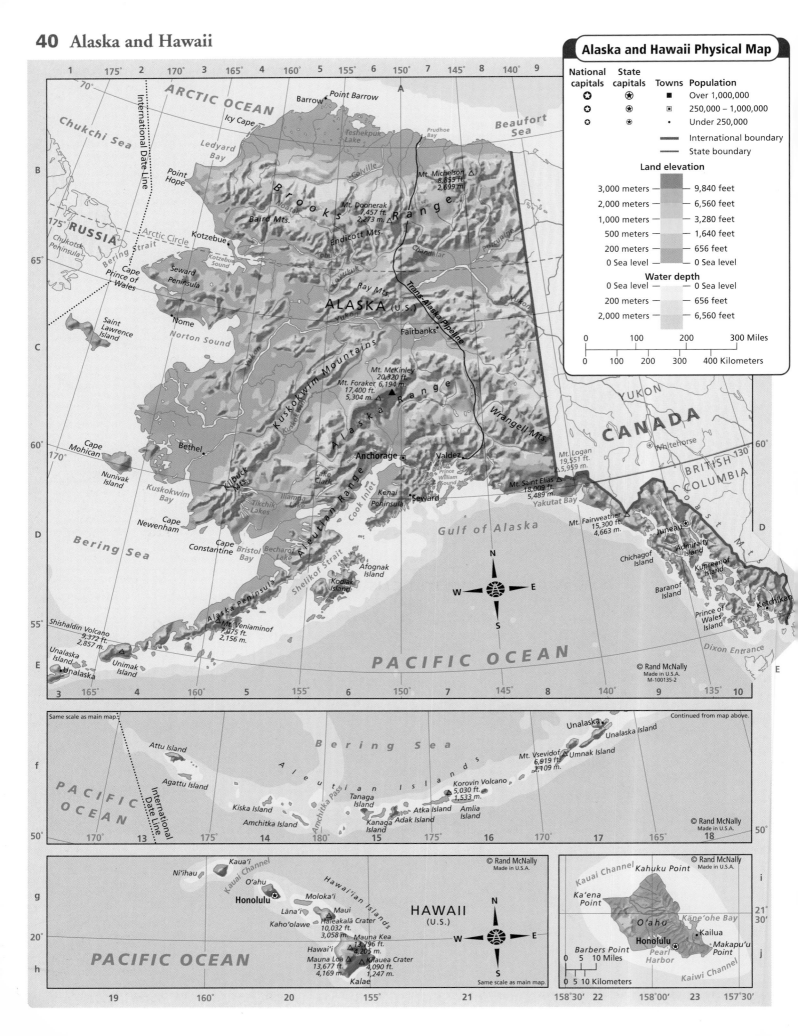

Alaska and Hawaii Physical Map

National capitals	State capitals	Towns	Population
✪	✪	■	Over 1,000,000
✪	✪	▣	250,000 – 1,000,000
✪	✪	•	Under 250,000

International boundary
State boundary

Land elevation
3,000 meters —	— 9,840 feet
2,000 meters —	— 6,560 feet
1,000 meters —	— 3,280 feet
500 meters —	— 1,640 feet
200 meters —	— 656 feet
0 Sea level —	— 0 Sea level

Water depth
0 Sea level —	— 0 Sea level
200 meters —	— 656 feet
2,000 meters —	— 6,560 feet

0   100   200   300 Miles
0 100 200 300 400 Kilometers

Main map labels

ARCTIC OCEAN
Chukchi Sea
International Date Line
Barrow · Point Barrow
Icy Cape
Teshekpuk Lake
Prudhoe Bay
Beaufort Sea
Ledyard Bay
Colville
Point Hope
Brooks Range
Mt. Michelson 8,855 ft. 2,699 m.
RUSSIA
Chukotsk Peninsula
Arctic Circle
Bering Strait
Kotzebue
Baird Mts.
Mt. Doonerak 7,457 ft. 2,273 m.
Endicott Mts.
Kobuk
Chandalar
Porcupine
Cape Prince of Wales
Seward Peninsula
Kotzebue Sound
Noatak
Ray Mts.
Trans-Alaska Pipeline
Yukon
Saint Lawrence Island
Nome
Norton Sound
Yukon
ALASKA (U.S.)
Fairbanks
Kuskokwim Mountains
Mt. McKinley 20,320 ft. 6,194 m.
Mt. Foraker 17,400 ft. 5,304 m.
Alaska Range
Wrangell Mts.
YUKON
CANADA
Cape Mohican
Bethel
Mt. Logan 19,551 ft. 5,959 m.
Whitehorse
BRITISH COLUMBIA
Nunivak Island
Kuskokwim Bay
Kilbuck Mts.
Lake Clark
Iliamna Lake
Anchorage
Valdez
Prince William Sound
Mt. Saint Elias 18,009 ft. 5,489 m.
Yakutat Bay
Cape Newenham
Tikchik Lakes
Kenai Peninsula
Seward
Cook Inlet
Cape Constantine
Bristol Bay
Becharof Lake
Aleutian Range
Shelikof Strait
Gulf of Alaska
Mt. Fairweather 15,300 ft. 4,663 m.
Chichagof Island
Juneau
Admiralty Island
Kupreanof Island
Bering Sea
Afognak Island
Kodiak Island
Baranof Island
Ketchikan
Alaska Peninsula
Mt. Veniaminof 7,075 ft. 2,156 m.
Prince of Wales Island
Shishaldin Volcano 9,372 ft. 2,857 m.
PACIFIC OCEAN
Dixon Entrance
Unalaska Island
Unalaska
Unimak Island
© Rand McNally
Made in U.S.A.
M-100135-2

Aleutian Islands inset
Same scale as main map.
Continued from map above.
Attu Island
Bering Sea
Unalaska
Unalaska Island
PACIFIC OCEAN
International Date Line
Agattu Island
Aleutian Islands
Mt. Vsevidof 6,919 ft. 2,109 m.
Umnak Island
Kiska Island
Amchitka Pass
Tanaga Island
Korovin Volcano 5,030 ft. 1,533 m.
Amchitka Island
Kanaga Island
Adak Island
Atka Island
Amlia Island
© Rand McNally
Made in U.S.A.

Hawaii inset
© Rand McNally
Made in U.S.A.
Ni'ihau
Kaua'i
Kauai Channel
O'ahu
Honolulu
Moloka'i
Lāna'i
Maui
Hawaiian Islands
HAWAII (U.S.)
Kaho'olawe
Haleakalā Crater 10,032 ft. 3,058 m.
Mauna Kea 13,796 ft. 4,205 m.
Hawai'i
Mauna Loa 13,677 ft. 4,169 m.
Kīlauea Crater 4,090 ft. 1,247 m.
Kalae
PACIFIC OCEAN
Same scale as main map.

O'ahu inset
© Rand McNally
Made in U.S.A.
Kauai Channel
Kahuku Point
Ka'ena Point
O'ahu
Kāne'ohe Bay
Kailua
Barbers Point
Honolulu
Pearl Harbor
Makapu'u Point
Kaiwi Channel
0 5 10 Miles
0 5 10 Kilometers

Location of Alaska and Hawaii

The states of Alaska and Hawaii are separated from the 48 conterminous states. Canada lies between Alaska and the other states. Hawaii is a chain of islands in the middle of the Pacific Ocean.

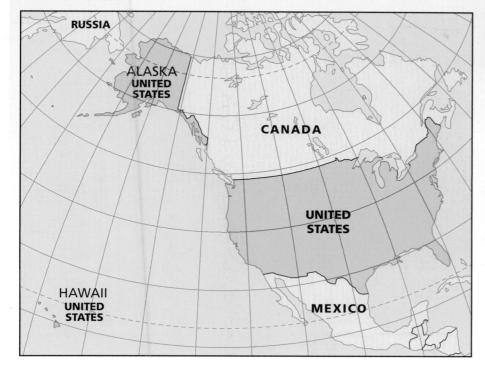

The United States annexed Hawaii in 1898. It became the 50th state in 1959. This photo shows the coast of Maui, the second-largest of the Hawai'ian islands.

The United States purchased the vast territory of Alaska from Russia in 1867. When Alaska became the 49th U.S. state in 1959, it increased the size of the country by nearly one-fifth.

Indian Reservations of the Conterminous United States

About 3 million Native Americans, or American Indians, live in the United States. About 22% live on or near reservations.

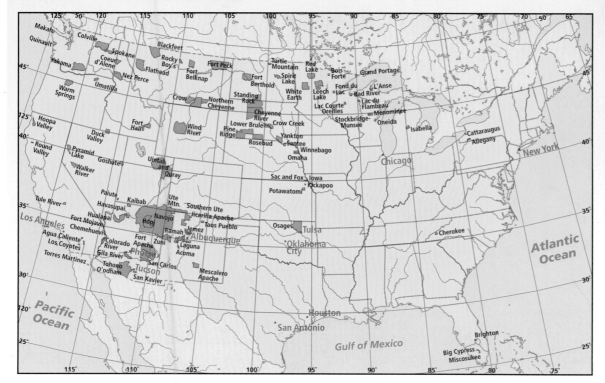

Pueblo Indian ruins in New Mexico reflect an ancient culture.

Navaso Reservation in Gallup, New Mexico

Ceremonial clothing at a powwow in North Dakota

Climate

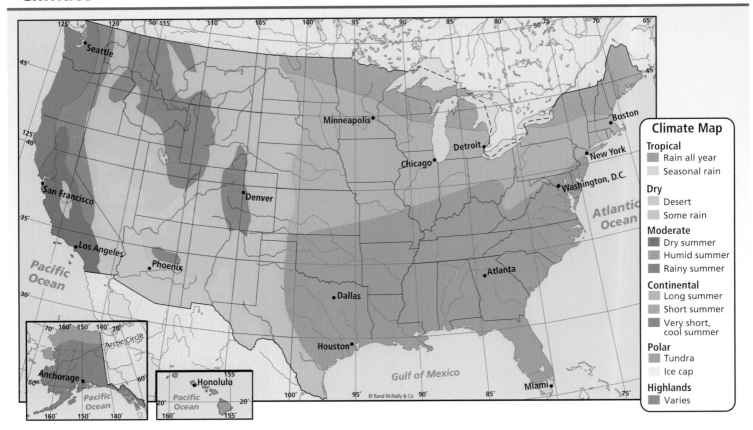

Climate Map

Tropical
- Rain all year
- Seasonal rain

Dry
- Desert
- Some rain

Moderate
- Dry summer
- Humid summer
- Rainy summer

Continental
- Long summer
- Short summer
- Very short, cool summer

Polar
- Tundra
- Ice cap

Highlands
- Varies

Economic Activities

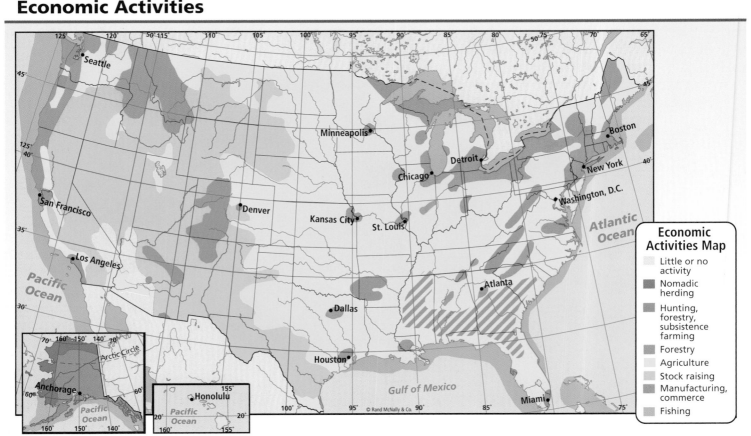

Economic Activities Map
- Little or no activity
- Nomadic herding
- Hunting, forestry, subsistence farming
- Forestry
- Agriculture
- Stock raising
- Manufacturing, commerce
- Fishing

Population

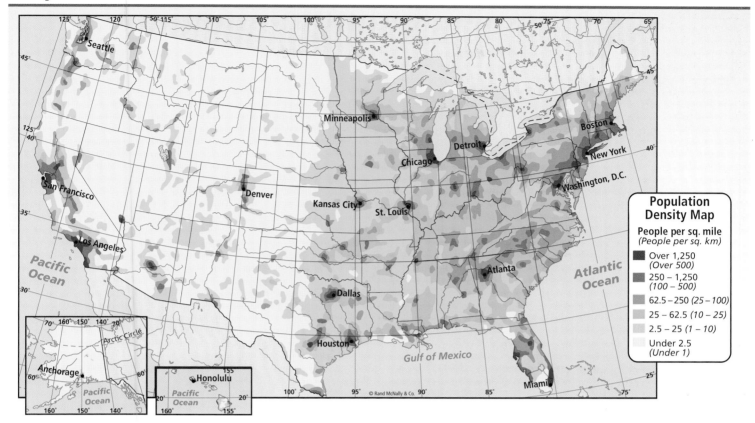

Population Density Map

People per sq. mile
(People per sq. km)

- Over 1,250 (Over 500)
- 250 – 1,250 (100 – 500)
- 62.5 – 250 (25 – 100)
- 25 – 62.5 (10 – 25)
- 2.5 – 25 (1 – 10)
- Under 2.5 (Under 1)

The United States has always been a nation of immigrants. It is one of the most culturally diverse countries in the world.

Approximately 81% of all Americans live in cities and towns.

Urban and Rural Population in the United States

1920

Rural 49% Urban 51%

2010

Rural 19% Urban 81%

City Landmarks

Many cities have famous landmarks, such as buildings, bridges, and monuments. How many of these landmarks, and their cities, can you name? The answers are at the bottom of the page.

1

2

3

4

5

6

Answers: 1. The Gateway Arch in St. Louis, Missouri 2. The Space Needle in Seattle, Washington 3. The Alamo in San Antonio, Texas 4. The Golden Gate Bridge in San Francisco, California 5. The Empire State Building in New York, New York 6. The Corn Palace in Mitchell, South Dakota

Environments

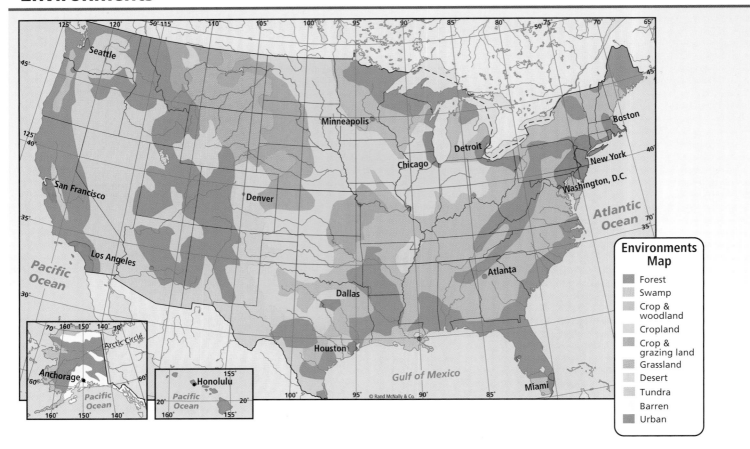

Environments Map

- Forest
- Swamp
- Crop & woodland
- Cropland
- Crop & grazing land
- Grassland
- Desert
- Tundra
- Barren
- Urban

© Rand McNally & Co.

Transportation

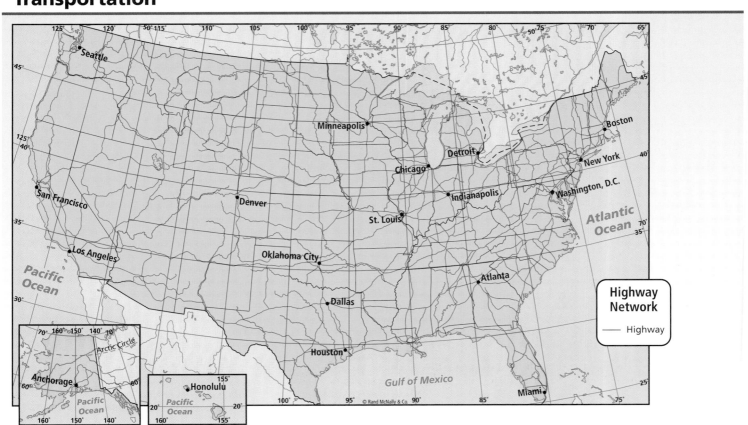

Highway Network

— Highway

© Rand McNally & Co.

United States Regions

The United States can be divided into regions in many different ways. The maps on this page show two different ways of grouping the states.

Map 1

Pacific

Rocky Mountains

Great Plains

Midwest

Northeast

Mid-Atlantic

Southwest

South

Map 2

Northwest

North Central

Midwest

Northeast

Mid-Atlantic

Alaska

Southwest

Southeast

South Central

Hawaii

There are many opinions about what to call the different regions. There are also many opinions about where the boundary lines between regions belong. What do you call the region where you live? Why?

The pages that follow show information about the regions shown on Map 2.

The Northeast Region

The Northeast Region was settled by people from Western Europe. In fact, the six states east of New York are known as New England. The Northeast was the site of five of the original 13 American colonies. Because much of the land is not suitable for farming, manufacturing has always been important in this region.

Vermont is known for its brilliant fall colors and its abundant dairy farms.

Every state in the Northeast Region except Vermont borders the Atlantic Ocean. This lighthouse is in Maine.

States of the Northeast Region

State	Land Area (square miles)	Population	Capital
Connecticut	4,842	3,574,097	Hartford
Maine	30,843	1,328,361	Augusta
Massachusetts	7,800	6,547,629	Boston
New Hampshire	8,953	1,316,470	Concord
New York	47,126	19,378,102	Albany
Rhode Island	1,034	1,052,567	Providence
Vermont	9,217	625,741	Montpelier

New York, New York, is the most populous city in the Northeast and in the United States.

The original Mayflower ship brought 102 passengers from England to Massachusetts in 1620. Today, visitors can tour this replica in Plymouth, Massachusetts.

Niagara Falls, in New York and Canada, provide hydroelectric power to the Northeast.

The Mid-Atlantic Region

The Mid-Atlantic Region is small in size but large in population. Oil, steel, and coal from this region fueled America's industry and power for many decades. Washington, D.C., the national capital, is not part of any state. The letters "D.C." stand for District of Columbia, a federal district sandwiched between Maryland and Virginia.

The Senate and House of Representatives meet in the U.S. Capitol Building in Washington, D.C.

Philadelphia, Pennsylvania, is the most populous city in the Mid-Atlantic region.

States of the Mid-Atlantic Region

State	Land Area (square miles)	Population	Capital
Delaware	1,949	897,934	Dover
Maryland	9,707	5,733,552	Annapolis
New Jersey	7,354	8,791,894	Trenton
Pennsylvania	44,743	12,702,379	Harrisburg
Virginia	39,490	8,001,024	Richmond
West Virginia	24,038	1,852,994	Charleston
Washington, D.C.*	61	601,723	— —

* The District of Columbia is not a state but a federal district.

Much of the land in the Mid-Atlantic Region is used for agriculture. This dairy farm is in Virginia.

Atlantic City, Cape May, and other resort cities draw millions of visitors to the New Jersey shore each year.

West Virginia is the most rural state in the Mid-Atlantic region. This quaint scene is in Babcock State Park.

The Southeast Region

This region stretches from the Atlantic Ocean in the east to the Mississippi River in the west. Its warm, humid climate is ideal for growing many crops, including cotton, sugarcane, and oranges. Manufacturing and tourism are also important to the region's economy.

The Great Smoky Mountains in Tennessee and North Carolina are part of the Appalachian mountain chain.

The space shuttle is launched at Cape Canaveral, Florida.

States of the Southeast Region

State	Land Area (square miles)	Population	Capital
Alabama	50,645	4,779,736	Montgomery
Florida	53,625	18,801,310	Tallahassee
Georgia	57,513	9,687,653	Atlanta
Mississippi	46,923	2,967,297	Jackson
North Carolina	48,618	9,535,483	Raleigh
South Carolina	30,061	4,625,364	Columbia
Tennessee	41,235	6,346,105	Nashville

Located near the southern tip of Florida, Miami Beach is a popular vacation spot.

Charleston, South Carolina, is noted for its historic homes and buildings.

Nashville, the capital of Tennessee, is known as Music City, U.S.A.

The Mississippi River is one of the nation's most important waterways.

The Midwest Region

With some of the best farmland in the world, the Midwest is an important agricultural region. Manufacturing also plays a big role in the region's economy. Large cities such as Chicago, Milwaukee, and Cleveland grew up as manufacturing centers along the shores of the Great Lakes.

Wisconsin is a leading producer of dairy products such as cheese and milk.

Chicago, Illinois, is the most populous city in the Midwest Region and the third most populous in the United States.

States of the Midwest Region

State	Land Area (square miles)	Population	Capital
Illinois	55,519	12,830,632	Springfield
Indiana	35,826	6,483,802	Indianapolis
Kentucky	39,486	4,339,367	Frankfort
Michigan	56,539	9,883,640	Lansing
Ohio	40,861	11,536,504	Columbus
Wisconsin	54,158	5,686,986	Madison

The northernmost part of this region is blanketed by forest and dotted with lakes. This photo shows Lake of the Clouds in northwestern Michigan.

The Ohio River is a major transportation artery. In this photo, a tugboat pushes barges past Cincinnati, Ohio.

Soybeans and corn are two of the most important crops grown in the Midwest Region. This soybean field is in northern Indiana.

The North Central Region

The land in the North Central Region is mostly flat or gently rolling, but it rises steadily from east to west. The climate changes across the region, too: it gradually becomes drier from east to west. Most of the land in the region is used for growing crops and for raising cattle.

The Mississippi River flows past downtown St. Louis and the graceful Gateway Arch.

Sunflowers grow on fertile prairie land in southeastern Minnesota.

States of the North Central Region

State	Land Area (square miles)	Population	Capital
Iowa	55,857	3,046,355	Des Moines
Kansas	81,759	2,853,118	Topeka
Minnesota	79,627	5,303,925	St. Paul
Missouri	68,741	5,998,927	Jefferson City
Nebraska	76,824	1,826,341	Lincoln
North Dakota	69,000	672,591	Bismarck
South Dakota	75,811	814,180	Pierre

Roughly nine-tenths of the land in Iowa is used for farming.

Abandoned farms are a common sight in the western half of this region. Some areas have been losing population for decades.

In the drier western half of this region, farmers make use of center-pivot irrigation systems, which tap into underground water.

In the Badlands of South Dakota, wind and water have sculpted the land into fantastic shapes.

The South Central Region

The South Central Region is similar to the North Central Region in many ways. From east to west, the land rises and the climate becomes drier. Farmers in this region grow crops such as wheat, cotton, and rice, and they raise cattle and sheep. Oil production is an important part of the economy.

The Dallas-Fort Worth area is the fourth-largest metropolitan area in the United States.

Swamps and bayous cover much of southern Louisiana.

States of the South Central Region

State	Land Area (square miles)	Population	Capital
Arkansas	52,035	2,915,918	Little Rock
Louisiana	43,204	4,533,372	Baton Rouge
Oklahoma	68,595	3,751,351	Oklahoma City
Texas	261,231	25,145,561	Austin

Raising livestock is an important economic activity in Texas and Oklahoma.

Canoeing, hiking, and other types of outdoor recreation are popular in the mountains of northwestern Arkansas.

The western half of this region is far more rugged than the eastern half. This photo is from Big Bend National Park in western Texas.

The Southwest Region

This region stretches from the Great Plains in the east to the Pacific Ocean in the west. In between are high mountains, rugged canyonlands, barren deserts, and areas of rich farmland. In recent decades, the population has boomed in many parts of the region. However, because of the dry climate, lack of water is a growing problem.

San Francisco, California, is located on one of the world's finest natural harbors.

Rock formations called "hoodoos" rise majestically in Utah's Bryce Canyon National Park.

States of the Southwest Region

State	Land Area (square miles)	Population	Capital
Arizona	113,594	6,392,017	Phoenix
California	155,799	37,253,956	Sacramento
Colorado	103,642	5,029,196	Denver
Nevada	109,781	2,700,551	Carson City
New Mexico	121,298	2,059,179	Santa Fe
Utah	82,169	2,763,885	Salt Lake City

Las Vegas is Nevada's economic center and largest city.

The Cliff Palace in Mesa Verde National Park, Colorado, was built by Native Americans more than 800 years ago.

The Grand Canyon in Arizona was carved by the Colorado River over the course of millions of years.

The Northwest Region

The Northwest Region, like the Southwest Region, extends from the Great Plains in the east to the Pacific Ocean in the west. Much of the land is mountainous and thinly populated. Many of the region's people live near its western edge, between the Pacific Ocean and the Cascade Range.

Seattle, Washington, is a technology center and an important trading partner with nations across the Pacific Ocean.

The jagged peaks of the Teton Range in western Wyoming were sculpted by glaciers.

States of the Northwest Region

State	Land Area (square miles)	Population	Capital
Idaho	82,643	1,567,582	Boise
Montana	145,546	989,415	Helena
Oregon	95,988	3,831,074	Salem
Washington	66,455	6,724,540	Olympia
Wyoming	97,093	563,626	Cheyenne

Ice-chiseled peaks soar skyward in Montana's Glacier National Park.

Some of the richest agricultural land in the United States is found along the Snake River in Idaho. This photo shows rows of potato plants.

Oregon's Crater Lake lies in the crater of a dormant volcano.

Alaska

Alaska lies hundreds of miles northwest of the "lower 48" states. It is by far the largest of the 50 states. However, because of its cold climate, it has a smaller population than all but three other states. Most Alaskans live in the southern part of the state. Alaska's landforms include broad plains, vast plateaus, and long mountain ranges.

Much of Alaska is pristine wilderness.

Soaring to 20,320 feet, Alaska's Mount McKinley is the highest peak in North America.

Anchorage is Alaska's most populous city.

Alaska has more than 40 active volcanoes. This photo shows the volcano that forms Augustine Island in the Cook Inlet.

North of the Brooks Range lies a coastal lowland that is home to enormous herds of caribou. This photo shows a caribou bull.

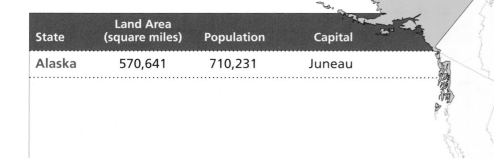

State	Land Area (square miles)	Population	Capital
Alaska	570,641	710,231	Juneau

CANADA

Hawaii

The islands that make up the state of Hawaii are located in the middle of the Pacific Ocean. The islands are actually the tops of volcanic mountains that rise from the ocean floor. Some of the volcanoes are still active. Because of Hawaii's warm, sunny climate, its beaches, and its spectacular scenery, the state is a popular destination for tourists from other states and from all over the world.

Honolulu is Hawaii's capital, most populous city, and main port. It stretches for about 10 miles along the coast of O'ahu.

Kilauea, located on the "Big Island" of Hawai`i, is one of the most active volcanoes in the world.

Hawaii's pleasant climate is a result of its location in the tropics, the fact that it is surrounded by ocean, and the moderating effect of trade winds.

Rugged cliffs rise thousands of feet above the Pacific Ocean along the Na Pali Coast on the island of Kaua'i.

Fertile volcanic soils and a tropical climate make Hawaii ideal for agriculture. This photo shows a taro field on the island of Kaua'i.

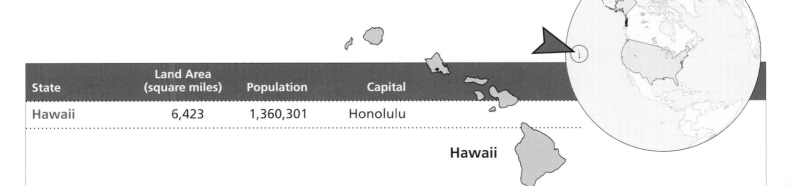

State	Land Area (square miles)	Population	Capital
Hawaii	6,423	1,360,301	Honolulu

Hawaii

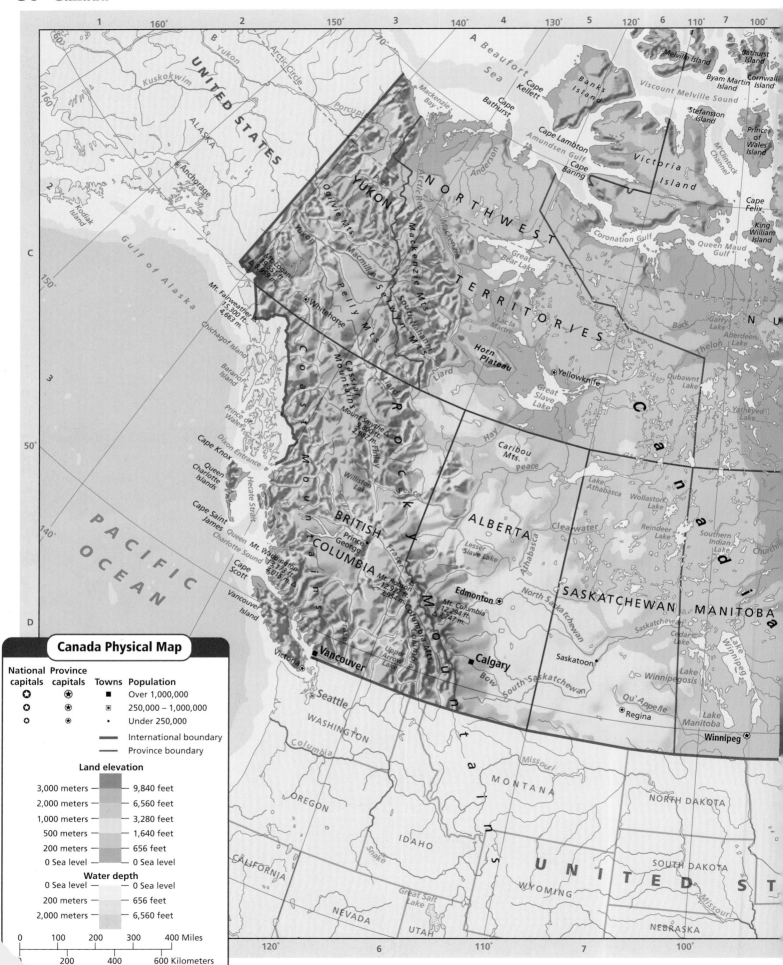

Canada Physical Map

National capitals	Province capitals	Towns	Population
✪	✪	■	Over 1,000,000
✪	✪	▣	250,000 – 1,000,000
✪	✪	•	Under 250,000

International boundary
Province boundary

Land elevation

3,000 meters	9,840 feet
2,000 meters	6,560 feet
1,000 meters	3,280 feet
500 meters	1,640 feet
200 meters	656 feet
0 Sea level	0 Sea level

Water depth

0 Sea level	0 Sea level
200 meters	656 feet
2,000 meters	6,560 feet

0   100   200   300   400 Miles

200   400   600 Kilometers

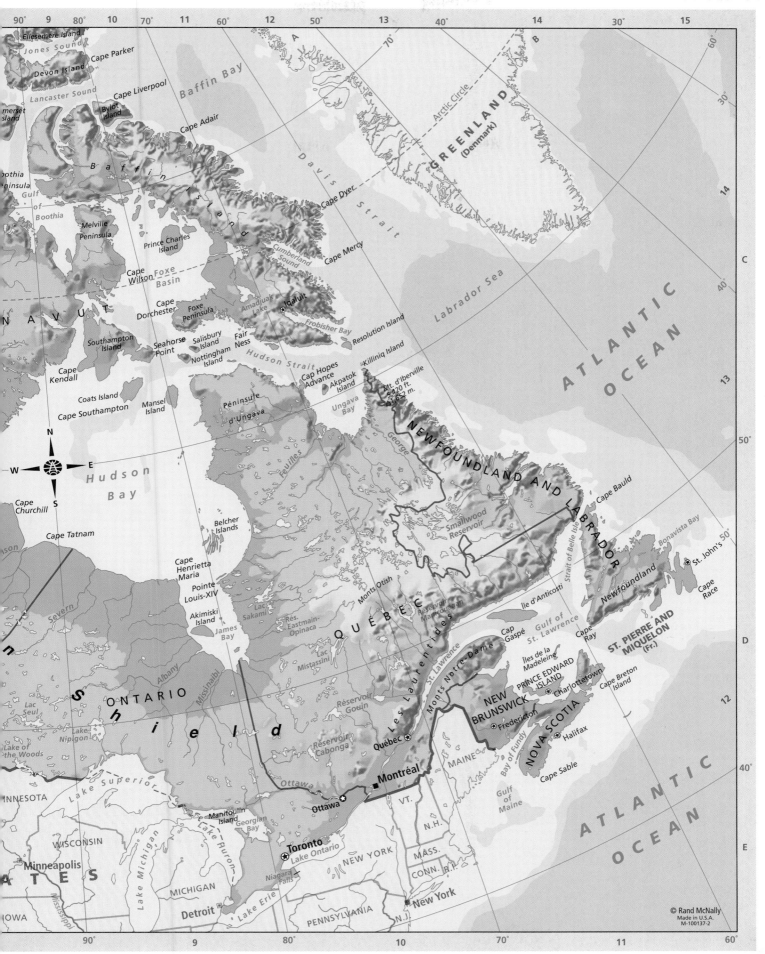

90°   9   80°   10   70°   11   60°   12   50°   13   40°   14   30°   15

Ellesmere Island
Jones Sound
Devon Island   Cape Parker
Lancaster Sound   Cape Liverpool
merset   *Bylot Island*
sland   Cape Adair
Boothia
ninsula   B a f f i n   I s l a n d   Baffin Bay
Gulf of Boothia
Melville Peninsula
Cape Wilson   Prince Charles Island
Foxe Basin   Cumberland Sound   Cape Mercy
Cape Dorchester
N A V U T   Foxe Peninsula   Amadjuak Lake   •Iqaluit
Southampton Island   Seahorse Point   Salisbury Island   Fair Ness   Frobisher Bay   Resolution Island
Cape Kendall   Nottingham Island
Coats Island   Mansel Island   Hudson Strait   Cap Hopes Advance   Killiniq Island
Cape Southampton   Péninsule d'Ungava   Ungava Bay   Akpatok Island   Mt. d'Iberville 5,420 ft. 1,652 m.

ATLANTIC OCEAN

GREENLAND (Denmark)

Arctic Circle

Davis Strait

Cape Dyer

Labrador Sea

Hudson Bay
N
W   E
S

Cape Churchill
Cape Tatnam
Belcher Islands
Cape Henrietta Maria
Pointe Louis-XIV
Akimiski Island
James Bay
Severn
Albany
Missinaibi
S h i e l d
ONTARIO
Lac Seul
Lake Nipigon
Lake of the Woods

Feuilles
George
Rès.
Réservoir Caniapiscau
N E W F O U N D L A N D   A N D   L A B R A D O R
Smallwood Reservoir
Cape Bauld
Strait of Belle Isle
Bonavista Bay
•St. John's
Newfoundland
Cape Race

Monts Otish
Lac Sakami
Rès. Eastmain-Opinaca
QUÉBEC
Lac Mistassini
Réservoir Gouin
Réservoir Cabonga
Réservoir Manicouagan
Monts Otish
Les Laurentides
Monts Notre-Dame
Île d'Anticosti
Gulf of St. Lawrence
Cap Gaspé
Cape Ray
ST. PIERRE AND MIQUELON (Fr.)
Cape Breton Island

Îles de la Madeleine
PRINCE EDWARD ISLAND
•Charlottetown
NEW BRUNSWICK
•Fredericton
Québec ✪
■Montréal
Ottawa ✪
Ottawa
MAINE
Bay of Fundy
NOVA SCOTIA
✪Halifax
Cape Sable
Gulf of Maine

VT.
N.H.
N.Y.

Manitoulin Island
Georgian Bay
Lake Huron
Toronto ✪
Lake Ontario
Niagara Falls
NEW YORK
MASS.
CONN. R.I.
N.J.

Minneapolis
WISCONSIN
MICHIGAN
Lake Michigan
Lake Erie
Detroit
PENNSYLVANIA
IOWA
T E S
Mississippi
MINNESOTA
Lake Superior

ATLANTIC OCEAN

•New York

90°   9   80°   10   70°   11   60°

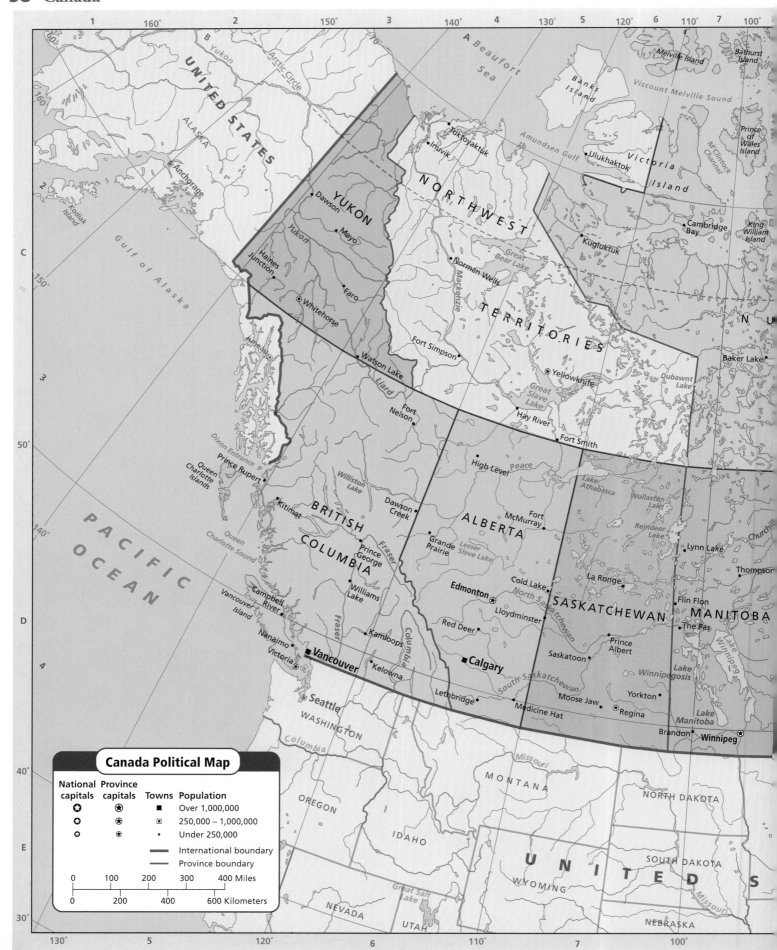

Canada Political Map

National capitals	Province capitals	Towns	Population
✪	✪	■	Over 1,000,000
✪	✪	▣	250,000 – 1,000,000
✪	✪	•	Under 250,000

━━━ International boundary
──── Province boundary

0   100   200   300   400 Miles
0   200   400   600 Kilometers

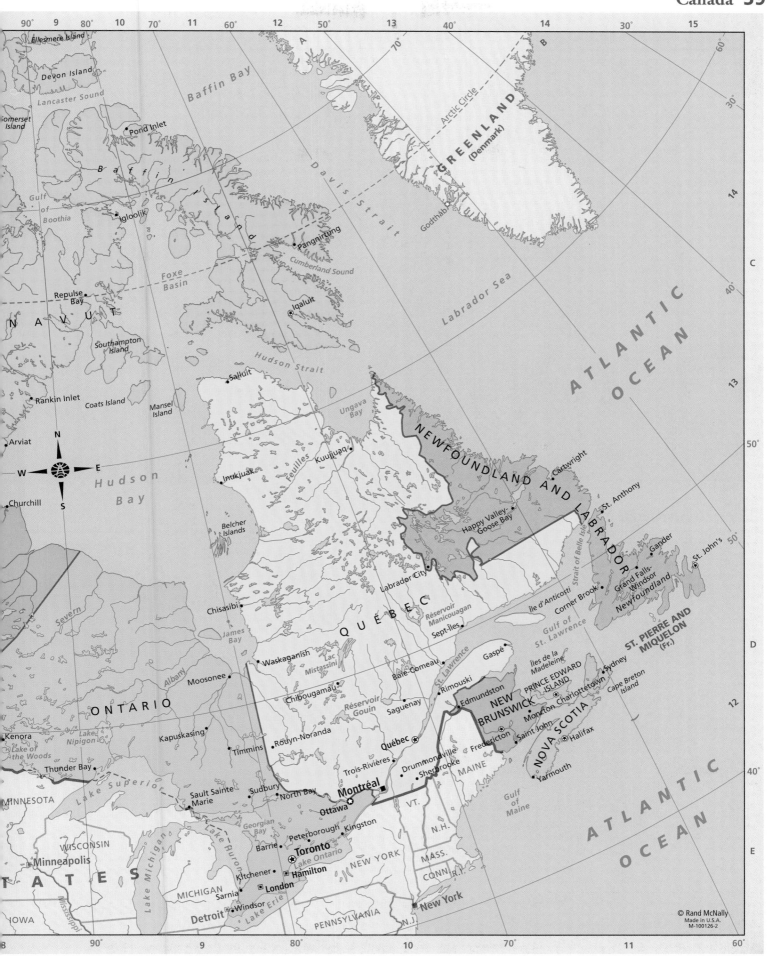

Ellesmere Island
Devon Island
Lancaster Sound
Somerset Island
Baffin Bay
Pond Inlet
Gulf of Boothia
Baffin Island
Igloolik
Foxe Basin
Cumberland Sound
Pangnirtung
Davis Strait
GREENLAND (Denmark)
Godthåb
Arctic Circle
ATLANTIC OCEAN
Repulse Bay
Iqaluit
Labrador Sea
N U N A V U T
Rankin Inlet
Coats Island
Mansel Island
Southampton Island
Hudson Strait
Salluit
Ungava Bay
Arviat
N
W — E
S
Hudson Bay
Inukjuak
Kuujjuaq
Feuilles
Cartwright
St. Anthony
Churchill
Belcher Islands
NEWFOUNDLAND AND LABRADOR
Happy Valley-Goose Bay
Strait of Belle Isle
Gander
St. John's
Grand Falls-Windsor
Newfoundland
Severn
James Bay
Chisasibi
Labrador City
Réservoir Manicouagan
Sept-Îles
Corner Brook
Île d'Anticosti
Gulf of St. Lawrence
ST. PIERRE AND MIQUELON (Fr.)
Albany
Moosonee
Waskaganish
Lac Mistassini
Baie-Comeau
QUÉBEC
Gaspé
Îles de la Madeleine
Sydney
Cape Breton Island
Chibougamau
Réservoir Gouin
Saguenay
Rimouski
Edmundston
PRINCE EDWARD ISLAND
Moncton
Charlottetown
ONTARIO
Kapuskasing
Rouyn-Noranda
NEW BRUNSWICK
NOVA SCOTIA
Kenora
Lake of the Woods
Lake Nipigon
Timmins
Québec
Drummondville
Fredericton
Saint John
Halifax
MINNESOTA
Thunder Bay
Lake Superior
Sudbury
North Bay
Trois-Rivières
Sherbrooke
MAINE
Yarmouth
Gulf of Maine
Sault Sainte Marie
Ottawa
Montréal
VT.
Georgian Bay
Peterborough
Kingston
N.H.
ATLANTIC OCEAN
WISCONSIN
Barrie
Lake Huron
Toronto
Lake Ontario
NEW YORK
MASS.
Minneapolis
Lake Michigan
Kitchener
Hamilton
CONN.
R.I.
MICHIGAN
Sarnia
London
Detroit
Windsor
Lake Erie
New York
IOWA
Mississippi
PENNSYLVANIA
N.J.
U N I T E D   S T A T E S

Population

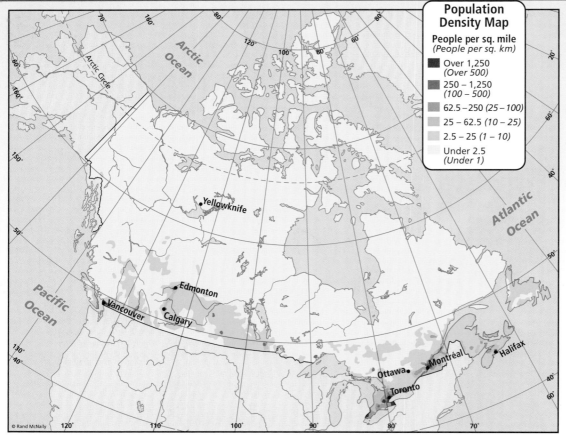

Population Density Map

People per sq. mile
(People per sq. km)

- Over 1,250 *(Over 500)*
- 250 – 1,250 *(100 – 500)*
- 62.5 – 250 *(25 – 100)*
- 25 – 62.5 *(10 – 25)*
- 2.5 – 25 *(1 – 10)*
- Under 2.5 *(Under 1)*

Approximately 90% of Canada's population lives within 100 miles of the United States border.

Canada's Population Growth since 1851

Canada's population grew rapidly in the twentieth century when many immigrants arrived from other countries.

Population in millions

Environments

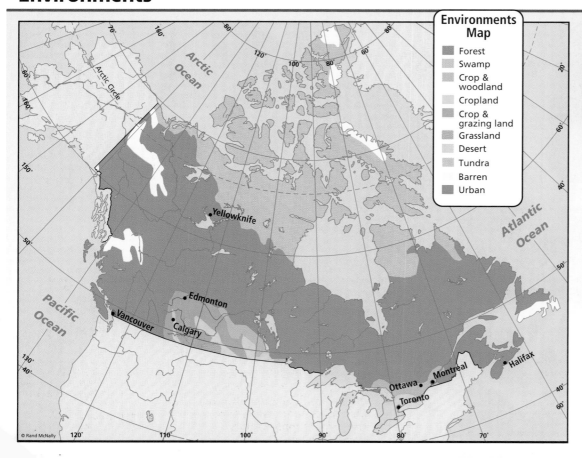

Environments Map

- Forest
- Swamp
- Crop & woodland
- Cropland
- Crop & grazing land
- Grassland
- Desert
- Tundra
- Barren
- Urban

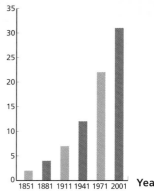

The Canadian Rocky Mountains extend through Alberta, British Columbia, and the Yukon territory.

The rocky plateau known as the Canadian Shield ends as headlands at the water's edge. Lighthouses help to guide ships away from the danger.

Transportation

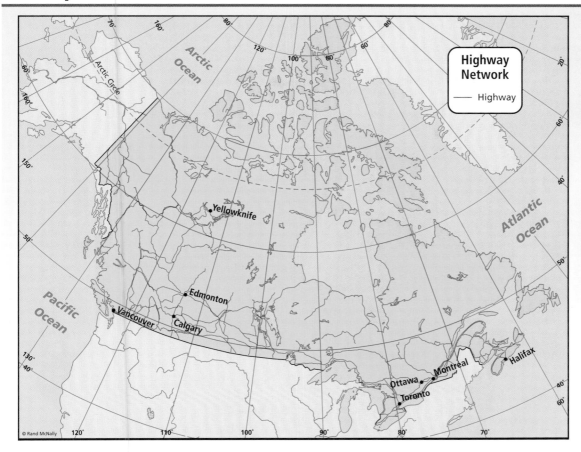

Scenic roads wind along the coasts of Canada's Maritime Provinces.

Canada's highways help to connect widely separated clusters of people across the country's vast expanse.

Economic Activities

Most of Canada's grain is grown in the "prairie provinces" of Alberta, Saskatchewan, and Manitoba.

Atlantic coast fishing is important to Canada's economy.

Toronto is Canada's financial center and the headquarters for many of the country's largest companies.

Canada's Economy

Services—such as banking, transportation, and government—account for more than two-thirds of Canada's economic output.

Agriculture 2%
Services 69%
Industry 29%

World Export of Oats

Oats are grains that are eaten by people and used for animal feed. On a global scale, Canada is a major oat producer. If Canadian weather interrupts oat growth, this can affect supply of oats across the world.

Russia 20%
Canada 15%
United States 7%
Poland 5%
Finland 4%
Germany 4%
Spain 3%
All other countries 58%

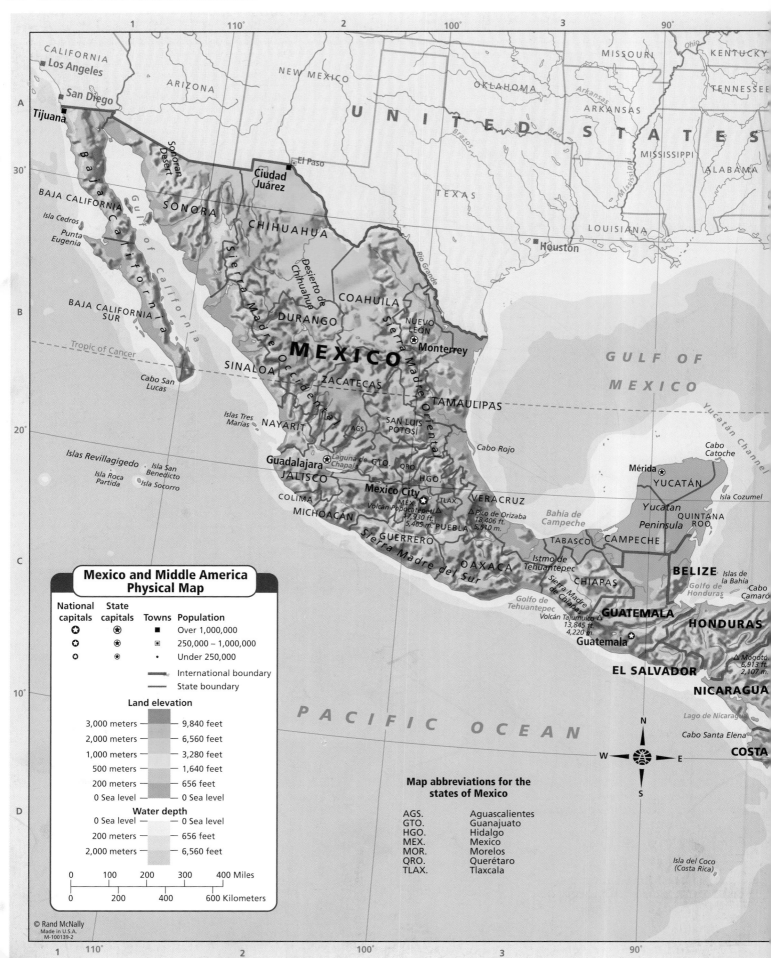

CALIFORNIA
Los Angeles
San Diego
Tijuana
ARIZONA
NEW MEXICO
MISSOURI
KENTUCKY
Ohio

UNITED STATES

OKLAHOMA
ARKANSAS
TENNESSEE

BAJA CALIFORNIA
Isla Cedros
Punta Eugenia
Sonoran Desert
SONORA
El Paso
Ciudad Juárez
CHIHUAHUA
TEXAS
MISSISSIPPI
ALABAMA
LOUISIANA
Houston

Baja California
BAJA CALIFORNIA SUR
Tropic of Cancer
Cabo San Lucas

Sierra Madre Occidental
Gulf of California
Desierto de Chihuahua
COAHUILA
DURANGO
NUEVO LEÓN
Monterrey
MEXICO
SINALOA
ZACATECAS
Sierra Madre Oriental
TAMAULIPAS

GULF OF MEXICO

Islas Tres Marías
NAYARIT
AGS
SAN LUIS POTOSÍ
Cabo Rojo

Yucatán Channel

Islas Revillagigedo
Isla San Benedicto
Isla Roca Partida
Isla Socorro
Guadalajara
Laguna de Chapala
JALISCO
COLIMA
MICHOACÁN
GTO.
QRO.
HGO.
Mexico City
MEX.
TLAX.
Volcán Popocatépetl
17,930 ft.
5,465 m.
PUEBLA
Pico de Orizaba
18,406 ft.
5,610 m.
VERACRUZ
GUERRERO
Sierra Madre del Sur
OAXACA
Istmo de Tehuantepec
Golfo de Tehuantepec
CHIAPAS
Sierra Madre de Chiapas
Volcán Tajumulco
13,845 ft.
4,220 m.
GUATEMALA
Guatemala

TABASCO
CAMPECHE
Bahía de Campeche
Cabo Catoche
Mérida
YUCATÁN
Yucatan Peninsula
QUINTANA ROO
Isla Cozumel
BELIZE
Islas de la Bahía
Golfo de Honduras
Cabo Camaró
HONDURAS
Mogotó
6,913 ft.
2,107 m.
EL SALVADOR
NICARAGUA
Lago de Nicaragua
Cabo Santa Elena
COSTA

PACIFIC OCEAN

N
W   E
S

Isla del Coco
(Costa Rica)

Mexico and Middle America Physical Map

National capitals	State capitals	Towns	Population
✪	✪	■	Over 1,000,000
✪	✪	▣	250,000 – 1,000,000
✪	✪	•	Under 250,000
			International boundary
			State boundary

Land elevation

3,000 meters	9,840 feet
2,000 meters	6,560 feet
1,000 meters	3,280 feet
500 meters	1,640 feet
200 meters	656 feet
0 Sea level	0 Sea level

Water depth

0 Sea level	0 Sea level
200 meters	656 feet
2,000 meters	6,560 feet

0   100   200   300   400 Miles
0   200   400   600 Kilometers

Map abbreviations for the states of Mexico

AGS.	Aguascalientes
GTO.	Guanajuato
HGO.	Hidalgo
MEX.	Mexico
MOR.	Morelos
QRO.	Querétaro
TLAX.	Tlaxcala

© Rand McNally
Made in U.S.A.
M-100139-2

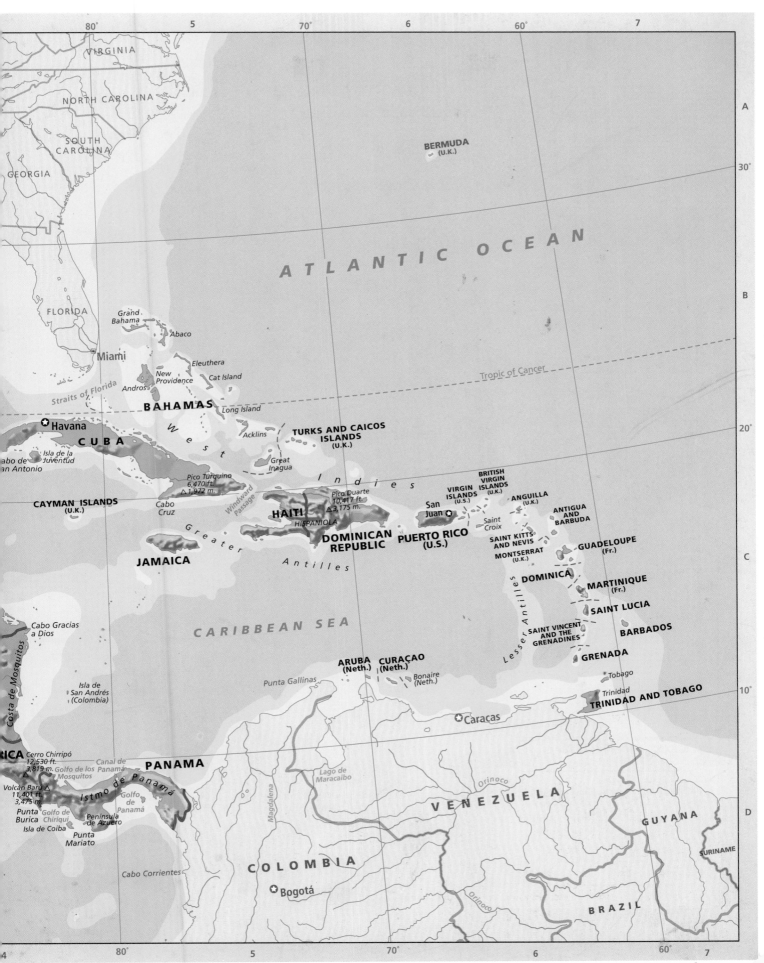

80°   5   70°   6   60°   7

VIRGINIA

NORTH CAROLINA

SOUTH
CAROLINA

GEORGIA

A

BERMUDA
(U.K.)

30°

A T L A N T I C   O C E A N

FLORIDA

B

Grand
Bahama

Abaco

Miami

Eleuthera

New
Providence   Cat Island

Andros

Straits of Florida

W   Tropic of Cancer

BAHAMAS   Long Island

20°

Havana   Acklins   **TURKS AND CAICOS
ISLANDS**
(U.K.)

CUBA

Isla de la
Juventud

Cabo de
San Antonio   Great
Inagua

e   *s*   *t*   *I* *n* *d* *i* *e* *s*

Pico Turquino
6,470 ft.
△1,972 m.

BRITISH
VIRGIN
ISLANDS
(U.K.)

Pico Duarte
10,417 ft.
△3,175 m.

VIRGIN
ISLANDS
(U.S.)   **ANGUILLA**
(U.K.)

CAYMAN ISLANDS
(U.K.)   Cabo
Cruz   Windward Passage   San
Juan   **ANTIGUA
AND
BARBUDA**

HAITI   Saint
Croix

HISPANIOLA   **SAINT KITTS
AND NEVIS**   **GUADELOUPE**
(Fr.)

G *r* *e* *a* *t* *e* *r*   **DOMINICAN
REPUBLIC**   **PUERTO RICO**
(U.S.)   **MONTSERRAT**
(U.K.)

C

JAMAICA   **DOMINICA**

A n t i l l e s   **MARTINIQUE**
(Fr.)

SAINT LUCIA

Cabo Gracias
a Dios

C A R I B B E A N   S E A   *L* *e* *s* *s* *e* *r*   **SAINT VINCENT
AND THE
GRENADINES**   **BARBADOS**

A *n* *t* *i* *l* *l* *e* *s*   **GRENADA**

Isla de
San Andrés
(Colombia)   **ARUBA**
(Neth.)   **CURAÇAO**
(Neth.)   Tobago

Bonaire
(Neth.)   Trinidad   **TRINIDAD AND TOBAGO**

Punta Gallinas   10°

Costa de Mosquitos

Caracas

RICA   Cerro Chirripó
12,530 ft.
3,819 m.   Canal de
Panamá
Golfo de los
Mosquitos   **PANAMA**   Lago de
Maracaibo

Orinoco

Volcán Barú △
11,401 ft.
3,475 m.   Istmo de Panamá   Golfo
de
Panamá   **V E N E Z U E L A**

Punta
Burica   Golfo de
Chiriquí   **GUYANA**

Isla de Coiba   Península
de Azuero

D

Punta
Mariato   Magdalena   **SURINAME**

C O L O M B I A

Cabo Corrientes   Bogotá

Orinoco   **B R A Z I L**

80°   5   70°   6   60°   7

4   5   6   7

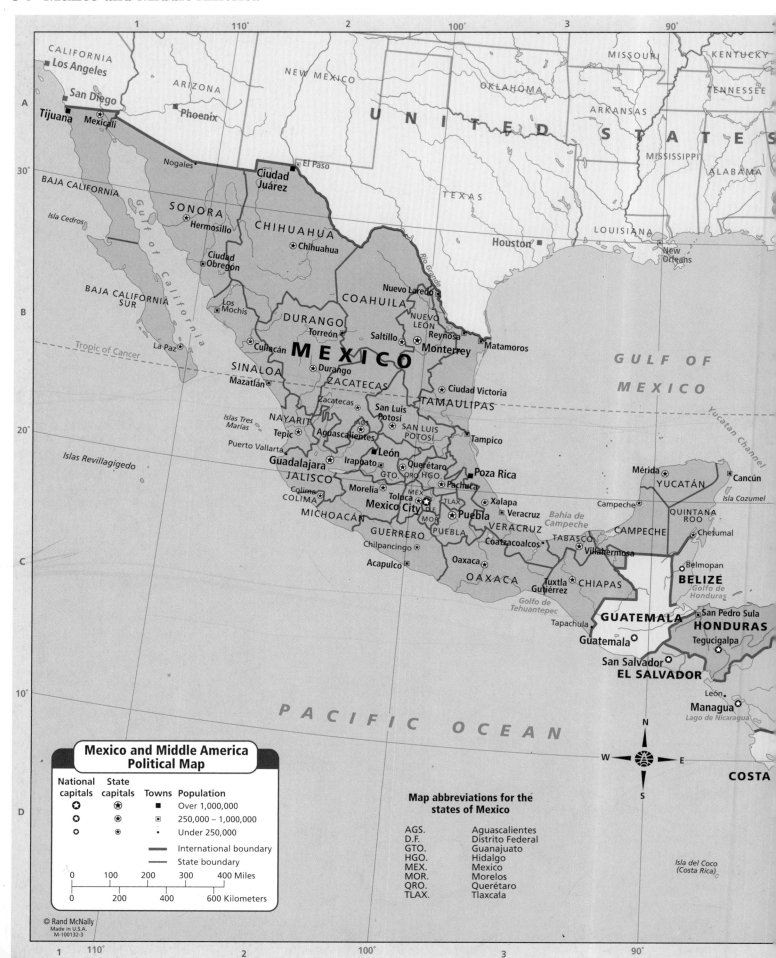

Mexico and Middle America Political Map

National capitals
- ✪ Over 1,000,000
- ✪ 250,000 – 1,000,000
- ✪ Under 250,000

State capitals
- ✪ Over 1,000,000
- ✪ 250,000 – 1,000,000
- ✪ Under 250,000

Towns / Population
- ■ Over 1,000,000
- ▣ 250,000 – 1,000,000
- • Under 250,000

─── International boundary
─── State boundary

0   100   200   300   400 Miles
0   200   400   600 Kilometers

© Rand McNally
Made in U.S.A.
M-100132-3

Map abbreviations for the states of Mexico

AGS.	Aguascalientes
D.F.	Distrito Federal
GTO.	Guanajuato
HGO.	Hidalgo
MEX.	Mexico
MOR.	Morelos
QRO.	Querétaro
TLAX.	Tlaxcala

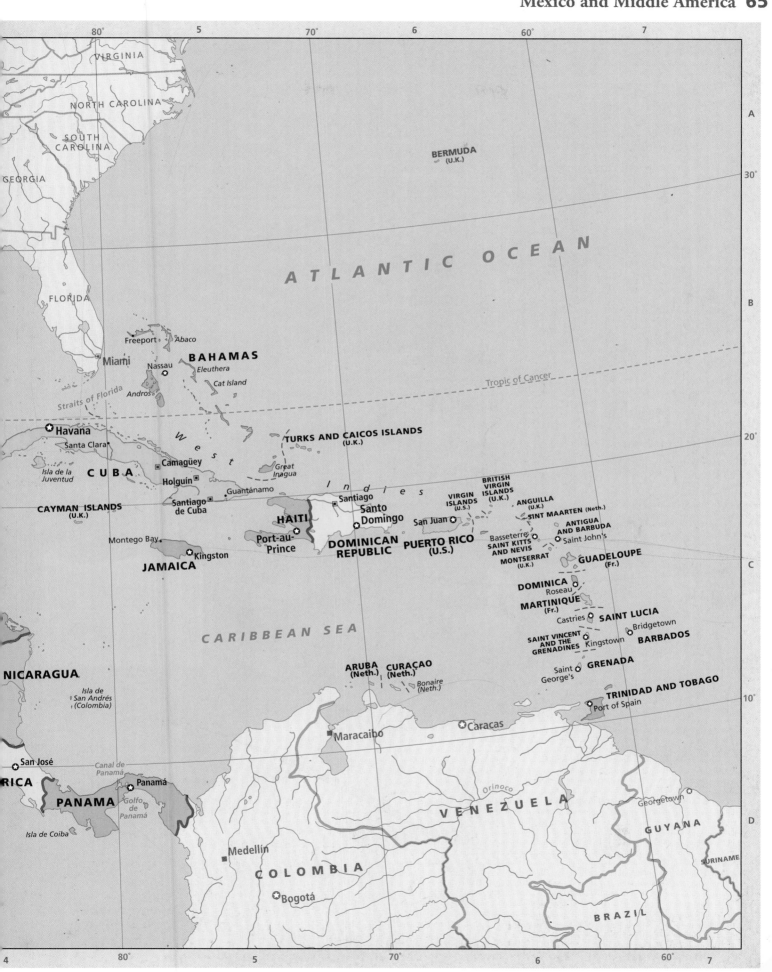

VIRGINIA

NORTH CAROLINA

SOUTH
CAROLINA

GEORGIA

FLORIDA

A

B

BERMUDA
(U.K.)

30°

A T L A N T I C   O C E A N

Tropic of Cancer

20°

Freeport *Abaco*

BAHAMAS

Miami
Nassau *Eleuthera*
Santa Clara *Cat Island*
Andros
Straits of Florida

◉ Havana

*Isla de la
Juventud*

CUBA

■ Camagüey

Holguín ■

Guantánamo

Santiago
de Cuba

CAYMAN ISLANDS
(U.K.)

Montego Bay

◉ Kingston

JAMAICA

W e s t

I n d i e s

*Great
Inagua*

TURKS AND CAICOS ISLANDS
(U.K.)

Santiago ■

HAITI

Port-au-
Prince

Santo
◉ Domingo

**DOMINICAN
REPUBLIC**

San Juan ◉

**VIRGIN
ISLANDS**
(U.S.)

**BRITISH
VIRGIN
ISLANDS**
(U.K.)

PUERTO RICO
(U.S.)

ANGUILLA
(U.K.)

SINT MAARTEN (Neth.)

**ANTIGUA
AND BARBUDA**
Basseterre ◉ Saint John's
**SAINT KITTS
AND NEVIS**

MONTSERRAT
(U.K.)

GUADELOUPE
(Fr.)

DOMINICA
Roseau

MARTINIQUE
(Fr.)
Castries **SAINT LUCIA**

Bridgetown

**SAINT VINCENT
AND THE
GRENADINES** Kingstown **BARBADOS**

C

C A R I B B E A N   S E A

NICARAGUA

*Isla de
San Andrés
(Colombia)*

ARUBA
(Neth.)

CURAÇAO
(Neth.)

*Bonaire
(Neth.)*

Saint
George's **GRENADA**

TRINIDAD AND TOBAGO
Port of Spain

10°

San José ◉

RICA

*Canal de
Panamá*

◉ Panamá

PANAMA

*Golfo
de
Panamá*

Isla de Coiba

■ Maracaibo

◉ Caracas

Orinoco

V E N E Z U E L A

Georgetown ◉

GUYANA

■ Medellín

SURINAME

D

C O L O M B I A

◉ Bogotá

B R A Z I L

Population

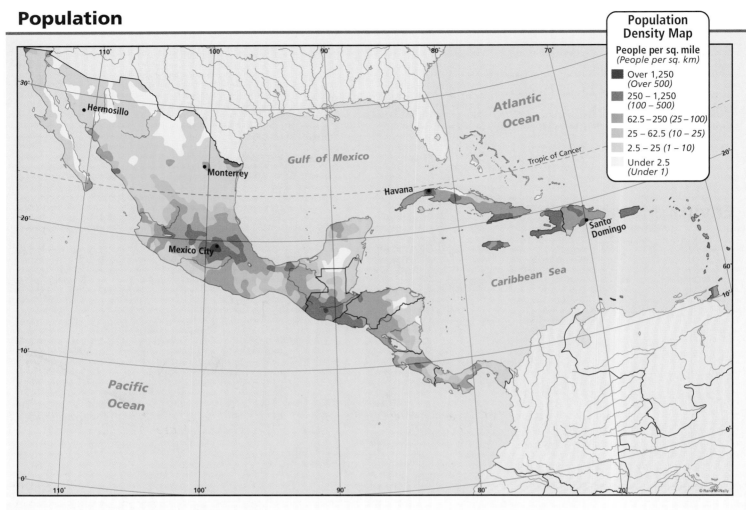

Population Density Map

People per sq. mile
(People per sq. km)

- Over 1,250 (Over 500)
- 250 – 1,250 (100 – 500)
- 62.5 – 250 (25 – 100)
- 25 – 62.5 (10 – 25)
- 2.5 – 25 (1 – 10)
- Under 2.5 (Under 1)

Comparing Urban and Rural Population

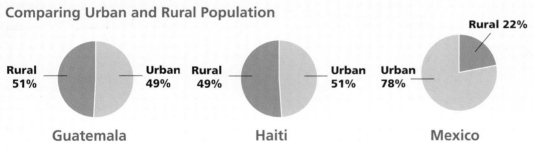

Rural 51% | Urban 49%
Guatemala

Rural 49% | Urban 51%
Haiti

Urban 78% | Rural 22%
Mexico

Mexico City is home to nearly one-fifth of Mexico's people.

A Timeline of Mexico City, Mexico

1500 B.C.E.
Native Americans settle in farm villages along the shores of Lake Texcoco.

1325 A.D.
Aztecs build the city of Tenochtitlán on an island in Lake Texcoco.

1521
Spaniards capture and destroy Tenochtitlán. They drain the lake, fill it with land, and build a new city they call Mexico City.

1960
Mexico City's population reaches 7 million.

1985
An earthquake does extensive damage, partly because Mexico City is built on soft, spongy soil.

2000
Mexico City's population reaches 18 million.

2010
Mexico City becomes the eighth richest metropolitan area in the world. The rating is based on the value of goods and services provided by the city in one year.

Economies

Per capita income is one way of measuring the relative wealth of countries. This graph compares the per capita income of six countries in Middle America. It shows how greatly wealth varies across the region, from relatively rich countries like Aruba to poor countries like Haiti.

Annual per capita income (in U.S. dollars)

Puerto Rico	$26,000
Aruba	$23,000
Mexico	$9,000
Cuba	$5,700
Jamaica	$4,900
Haiti	$600

0   $5,000 $10,000 $15,000 $20,000 $25,000 $30,000

Environments

Cactuses grow in the hot, dry climate of Baja California, Mexico.

Tropical rain forest covers much of Central America.

Palm trees flourish in the warm climate of the Caribbean Sea.

Transportation

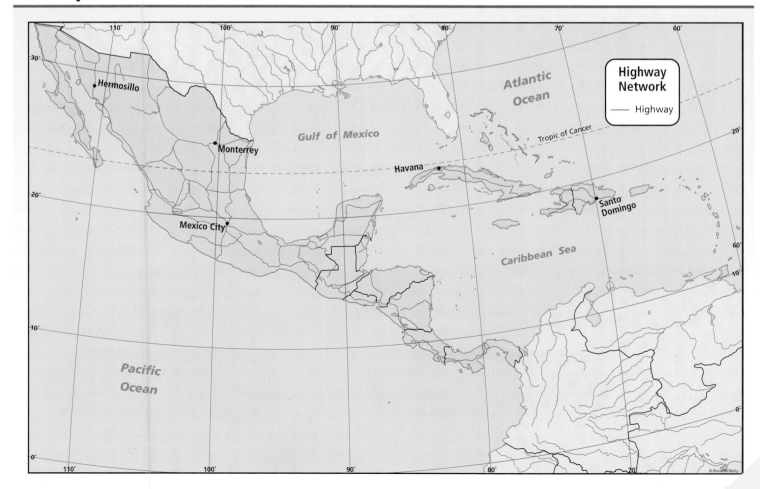

South America

South America is a continent of extremes. The Andes Mountains stretch 4,500 miles (7,200 kilometers) from north to south. They form the longest mountain chain in the world. Lake Titicaca, on the Peru-Bolivia border, is the highest lake in the world used for transportation. Arica, Chile, experienced the longest dry period ever recorded: No rain fell there for more than 14 years!

The Amazon River has the greatest volume of water of any river in the world. The Amazon discharges so much water into the Atlantic that it changes the color of the ocean's water for more than 100 miles (160 kilometers) off the shore.

Most South Americans live in cities that are major ports or are near major ports. São Paulo and Rio de Janeiro, Brazil, and Buenos Aires, Argentina, are among the world's largest cities. Altogether, almost 367 million people live in South America.

Iguassu Falls on the Brazil-Argentina border is among the most spectacular sights in South America.

Colorful buildings in Buenos Aires, Argentina

Giant tortoises on Ecuador's Galapagos Islands

A Historical Look At South America

Circa A.D. 600

Tiahuanaco civilization prospers along the shore of Lake Titicaca.

1498

Christopher Columbus reaches the Orinoco River.

The Inca Empire controls the Andes and the Pacific Coast.

1438–1535

The Portuguese establish sugar plantations in Brazil.

1530s

Rain Forests

A rain forest is a dense forest that receives at least 100 inches (250 centimeters) of rain a year. The Amazon rain forest is rich in plant and animal life, and new species are discovered almost daily. Scientists have learned that many of the plants can be used to produce life-saving drugs.

However, the rain forest is becoming smaller. Mining, logging, and industrial developments such as hydro-electric factories, are attracting people to the rain forest. From 2000 to 2010, the Amazon population has grown 23%. These people are looking for a place to work, and they also need a place to live. As a result, land is cleared of trees and other plants. Clearing and settling the land lead to deforestation. Nearly 20% of rain forest has been lost to deforestation.

Did You Know?

The Amazon River is the world's largest river by volume. Some scientists believe that this river is the longest river in the world, too. But other scientists believe that the Nile River is the longest.

Sights of the Andes Mountains

More than 40 peaks in the Andes rise 20,000 feet (6,000 meters) or higher. Mining is important in the Andes, and tourism is a growing industry.

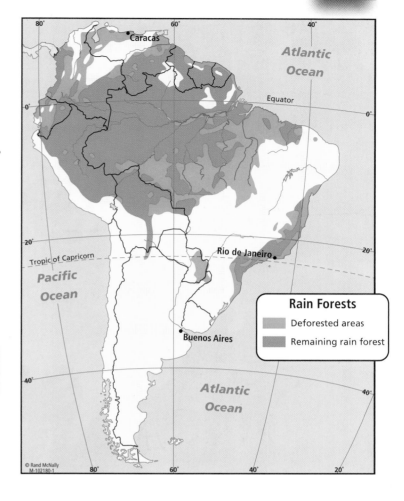

Rain Forests
- Deforested areas
- Remaining rain forest

The ancient Incan city of Machu Picchu, Peru

Lake Titicaca on the Peru-Bolivia border

A jagged peak along the Argentina-Chile border

The South American llama, a relative of the camel

1580

Spaniards found the city of Buenos Aires in Argentina.

The first coffee plantation is established in Brazil.
1726

2004

South America's population reaches 365 million.

Brazil establishes the world's largest rain forest reserve.
2006

South America Physical Map

National capitals
- ✪ (symbol) Over 1,000,000
- ✪ (symbol)
- ✪ (symbol)

Towns **Population**
- ■ Over 1,000,000
- ▣ 250,000 – 1,000,000
- • Under 250,000
- —— International boundary

Land elevation

3,000 meters	9,840 feet
2,000 meters	6,560 feet
1,000 meters	3,280 feet
500 meters	1,640 feet
200 meters	656 feet
0 Sea level	0 Sea level

Water depth

0 Sea level	0 Sea level
200 meters	656 feet
2,000 meters	6,560 feet

0 200 400 600 800 1000 Miles
0 300 600 900 1200 1500 Kilometers

© Rand McNally
Made in U.S.A.
M-100306- -1-1-1

South America Political Map

National capitals	Towns	Population
✪	■	Over 1,000,000
✪	◨	250,000 – 1,000,000
✪	•	Under 250,000
	▬▬	International boundary

0	200	400	600	800	1000 Miles
0	300	600	900	1200	1500 Kilometers

© Rand McNally
Made in U.S.A.
M-100129-2

Natural Hazards

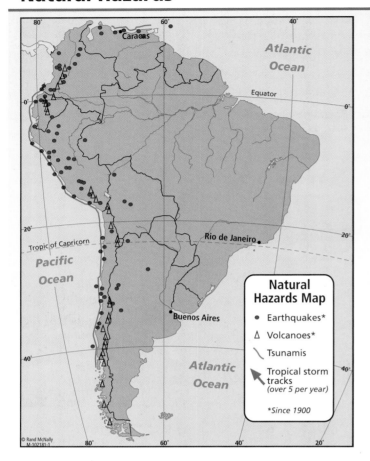

Natural Hazards Map

- • Earthquakes*
- △ Volcanoes*
- \ Tsunamis
- ↖ Tropical storm tracks *(over 5 per year)*

*Since 1900

Climate

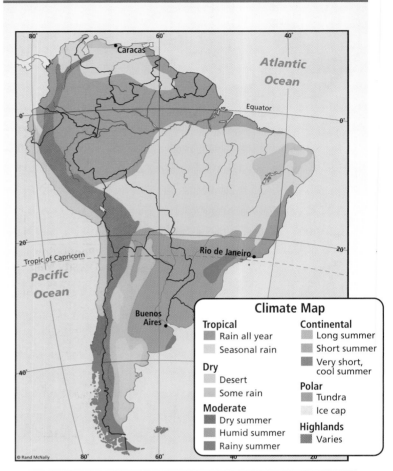

Climate Map

Tropical
- Rain all year
- Seasonal rain

Dry
- Desert
- Some rain

Moderate
- Dry summer
- Humid summer
- Rainy summer

Continental
- Long summer
- Short summer
- Very short, cool summer

Polar
- Tundra
- Ice cap

Highlands
- Varies

Environments

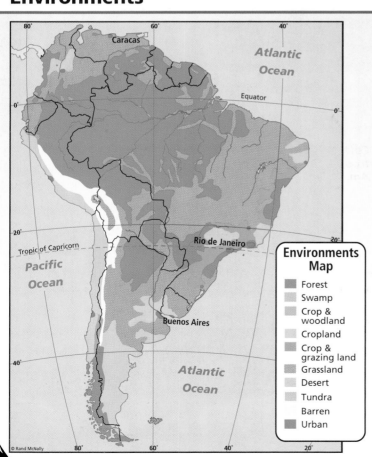

Environments Map
- Forest
- Swamp
- Crop & woodland
- Cropland
- Crop & grazing land
- Grassland
- Desert
- Tundra
- Barren
- Urban

The Amazon rain forest supports almost half of Earth's animal and plant species.

What If?

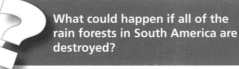

What could happen if all of the rain forests in South America are destroyed?

Population

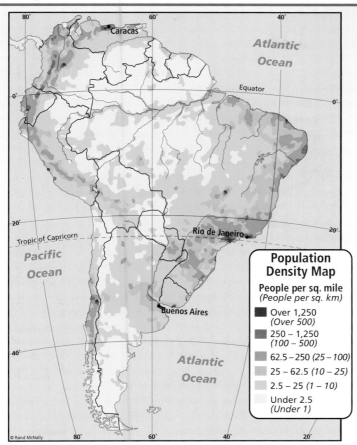

Population Density Map
People per sq. mile
(People per sq. km)
- Over 1,250 (Over 500)
- 250 – 1,250 (100 – 500)
- 62.5 – 250 (25 – 100)
- 25 – 62.5 (10 – 25)
- 2.5 – 25 (1 – 10)
- Under 2.5 (Under 1)

Most Brazilians live in large cities such as Rio de Janeiro.

Roughly three out of five people living in Brazil are under the age of 29.

Did You Know?

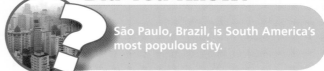

São Paulo, Brazil, is South America's most populous city.

Cusco, Peru, was once capital of the Incan empire.

The forest in the Amazon River Basin is so thick in parts that sunlight cannot reach the ground.

Economic Activities

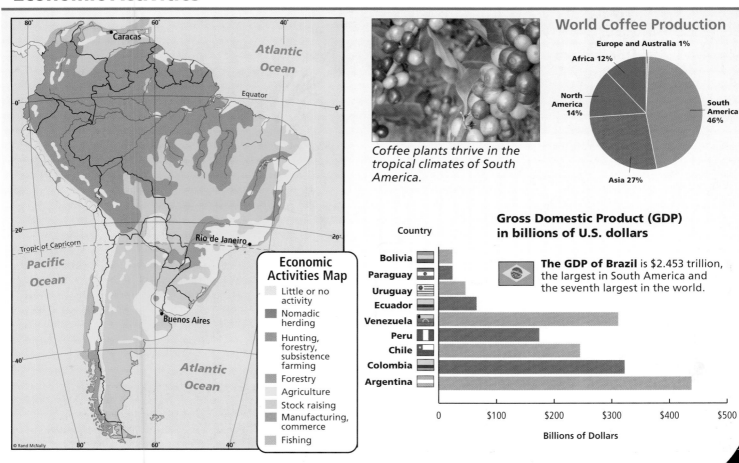

Economic Activities Map
- Little or no activity
- Nomadic herding
- Hunting, forestry, subsistence farming
- Forestry
- Agriculture
- Stock raising
- Manufacturing, commerce
- Fishing

Coffee plants thrive in the tropical climates of South America.

World Coffee Production
- Europe and Australia 1%
- Africa 12%
- North America 14%
- South America 46%
- Asia 27%

Gross Domestic Product (GDP) in billions of U.S. dollars

Country

Bolivia
Paraguay
Uruguay
Ecuador
Venezuela
Peru
Chile
Colombia
Argentina

| 0 | $100 | $200 | $300 | $400 | $500 |

Billions of Dollars

The GDP of Brazil is $2.453 trillion, the largest in South America and the seventh largest in the world.

Europe

Do you know what a *lago* is? A *lac*? A *loch*? These are just some of the words for "lake" in Europe. Europe is the world's second-smallest continent, but it has many countries and many languages.

Only the giant continents of Asia and Africa have more people than Europe. Because more than 729,000,000 live in the small continent of Europe, it is one of the most densely populated regions in the world.

The two smallest countries in the world are in Europe. Vatican City and Monaco are each less than one square mile (2.6 square kilometers) in size.

In recent decades, there have been great changes in Europe. East and West Germany were reunited in 1990 after being separated for 45 years. In 1991, the Soviet Union split up into 15 different countries. The following year, Czechoslovakia peacefully divided into two new countries: the Czech Republic and Slovakia.

Slovenia, Croatia, Macedonia, and Bosnia and Herzegovina broke away from Yugoslavia in 1991-92 to become independent countries. In 2003, Yugoslavia changed its name to Serbia and Montenegro. Then, in 2006, Montenegro split from Serbia to become an independent country. In 2008, a region known as Kosovo declared its independence from Serbia.

Prague, Czech Republic

Church in the Alps of Austria

Hilltop village in Spain

Donkey and farmhouse, Aran Islands, Ireland

Did You Know?

A Historical Look At Europe

Circa 2200 B.C.E.
Erecting of Stonehenge pillars begins in Great Britain.

753 B.C.E.

Rome is founded.

The first recorded Olympic Games are held in Greece.

776 B.C.E.

Iceland is settled by Norse seafarers.

A.D. 874

The European Union

Twenty-seven nations have joined the European Union to form a single, powerful market for business and trade.

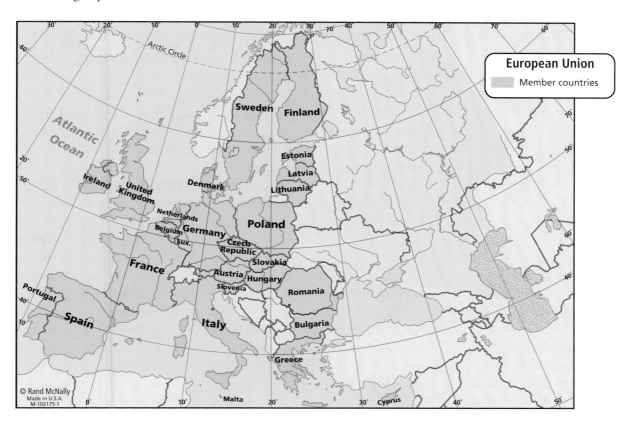

European Union
☐ Member countries

© Rand McNally
Made in U.S.A.
M-102175-1

The headquarters of the European Union is in Brussels, Belgium.

Some countries of the European Union use the euro as their currency.

Because Europe has so many languages, there are 23 official languages of the European Union.

The European Union has its own passports. Citizens of all countries can move freely around the entire area.

1163–1200

The great gothic Notre Dame Cathedral is built in Paris.

Circa 1750

The Industrial Revolution begins in England.

The period known as the Renaissance marks a rebirth in art and science.

1300s–1500s

Romania and Bulgaria join the European Union.

2007

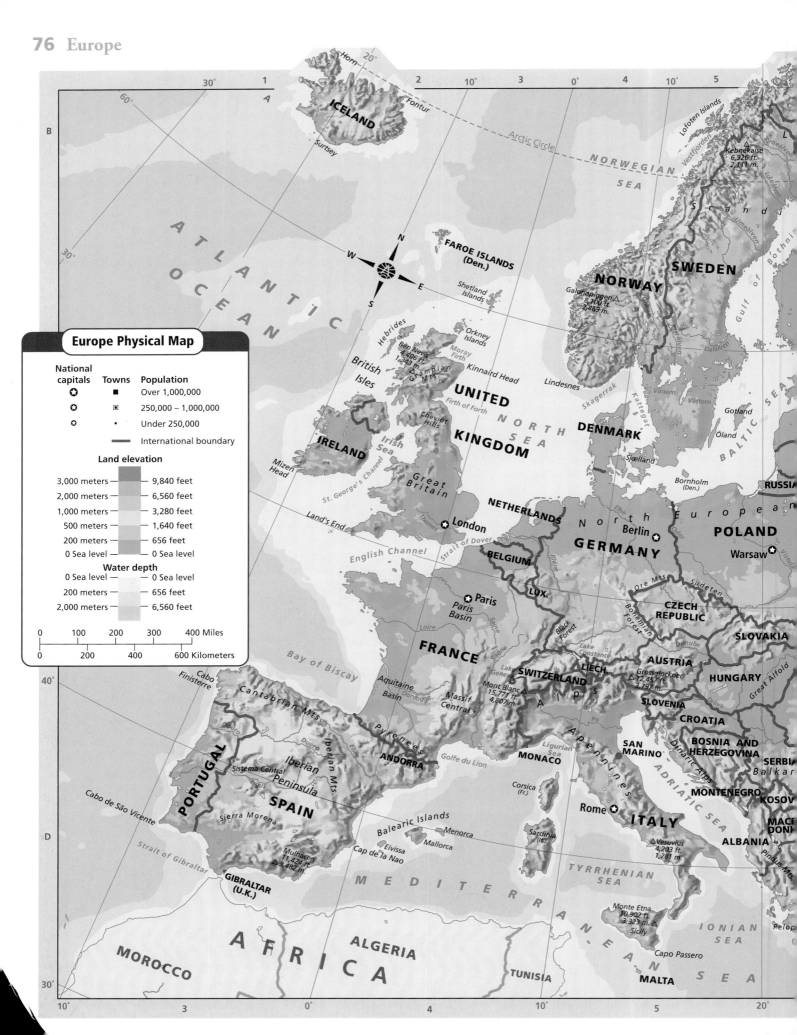

Europe Physical Map

National capitals ✪ ⊕ ✲
Towns ■ ⊡ •
Population
Over 1,000,000
250,000 – 1,000,000
Under 250,000
—— International boundary

Land elevation
3,000 meters	9,840 feet
2,000 meters	6,560 feet
1,000 meters	3,280 feet
500 meters	1,640 feet
200 meters	656 feet
0 Sea level	0 Sea level

Water depth
0 Sea level	0 Sea level
200 meters	656 feet
2,000 meters	6,560 feet

0 100 200 300 400 Miles
0 200 400 600 Kilometers

ICELAND
Horn
Fontur
Surtsey

FAROE ISLANDS (Den.)
Shetland Islands

NORWEGIAN SEA
Arctic Circle

Lofoten Islands
Vestfjorden
Kebnekaise 6,926 ft. 2,111 m.

SWEDEN
Scandi
Gulf of Bothnia

Galdhøpiggen 8,100 ft. 2,469 m.

ATLANTIC OCEAN

Hebrides
Orkney Islands
Ben Nevis 4,406 ft. 1,343 m.
Grampian Mts.
Moray Firth
Kinnaird Head
Lindesnes
Skagerrak
Kattegat
Vänern
Vättern
Gotland
Öland

British Isles
UNITED
Firth of Forth
Cheviot Hills
NORTH SEA
DENMARK
Sjælland
Bornholm (Den.)
BALTIC SEA

IRELAND
Irish Sea
KINGDOM
Great Britain
St. George's Channel
Land's End
NETHERLANDS
Nor th European
Berlin
RUSSIA
POLAND
Warsaw

Mizen Head
London
English Channel
Strait of Dover
BELGIUM
GERMANY
Rhine
Elbe
Oder

Paris
Paris Basin
Seine
LUX.
Black Forest
Ore Mts.
Sudeten
CZECH REPUBLIC
Bohemian Forest
Danube
SLOVAKIA

Bay of Biscay
Loire
FRANCE
Lake Constance
AUSTRIA
Grossglockner 12,457 ft. 3,797 m.
HUNGARY
Great Alföld

Aquitaine Basin
Dordogne
Massif Central
Saône
SWITZERLAND
Lake Geneva
Mont Blanc 15,771 ft. 4,807 m.
Alps
LIECH.
SLOVENIA
Drava
CROATIA

Cabo Finisterre
Cantabrian Mts.
Pyrenees
ANDORRA
Golfe du Lion
Rhône
Po
Apennines
Ligurian Sea
SAN MARINO
Dinaric Alps
BOSNIA AND HERZEGOVINA
SERBIA
Balkan

PORTUGAL
Duero
Ebro
Iberian Mts.
Sistema Central
Tagus
Iberian Peninsula
SPAIN
Sierra Morena
MONACO
Corsica (Fr.)
MONTENEGRO
KOSOVO
MACEDONI

Cabo de São Vicente
Mulhacén 11,424 ft. 3,482 m.
Balearic Islands
Eivissa
Mallorca
Menorca
Cap de la Nao
Sardinia (It.)
Rome
ITALY
Vesuvius 4,203 ft. 1,281 m.
ALBANIA
ADRIATIC SEA
Pindus Mts.

Strait of Gibraltar
GIBRALTAR (U.K.)
MEDITERRANEAN
Monte Etna 10,902 ft. 3,323 m.
Sicily
Capo Passero
TYRRHENIAN SEA
IONIAN SEA
Pelop

MOROCCO
AFRICA
ALGERIA
TUNISIA
MALTA
SEA

70°   7   40°   8   50°   9   60°   10   70°   11   80°

land

■ Murmansk

Kola
Peninsula

Ponoy

FINLAND

WHITE SEA

Mezen'

Timan Ridge

Pechora

Gora Narodnaya △
6,214 ft.
1,894 m.

Ob'

Irtysh

ASIA

B

via

Severnaya Dvina

Onega

Sukhona

Severnyye Uvaly
(Hills)

Ural Mountains

Kama

Kama
Resevoir

80°

*Lake
Onega*

Lake
Ladoga

R U S S I A

Gorki
Res.

60°

50°

ulf of Finland

STONIA

Lake
Peipus

*Rybinsk
Res.*

Volga

Kuybyshev
Res.

Aral Sea

70°

LATVIA

Valdai
Hills

☆ Moscow

Oka

Volgograd
Res.

Kuybyshev
Res.

C

THUANIA

Central
Russian
Upland

Oka-Don Plain

Don

Khopr

Volga Upland

Volga

Ural

KAZAKHSTAN

UZBEKISTAN

Amu Darya

P l a i n

Neman

BELARUS

Pryp'jac'

Dnieper Lowland

Dnieper

Donets Basin

*Tsymlyansk
Res.*

Volga

Caspian Depression

Kiev ☆

UKRAINE

Dniester

Caspian Depression

40°

MOLDOVA

Sea of Azov

C A S P I A N

TURKMENISTAN

60°

arpathian Mts.

OMANIA

Crimean
Peninsula

C a u c a s u s

GEORGIA

AZERBAIJAN

S E A

nsylvanian Alps

Gora El'brus
18,510 ft.
5,642 m.

ARMENIA

AZER.

Danube

Peninsula

B L A C K   S E A

BULGARIA

D

Rhodope Mts

İstanbul ■

IRAN

Sea of
Marmara

Mt. Olympus
,570 ft.
,917 m.

TURKEY

Tigris

AEGEAN SEA

GREECE

IRAQ

esus

Sea of Crete

Rhodes

CYPRUS

SYRIA

Euphrates

30°

LEBANON

© Rand McNally
Made in U.S.A.
M-100138-3

Crete

6   30°   7   40°   8   50°   9

Europe Political Map

National capitals	State capitals	Towns	Population
✪	✪	■	Over 1,000,000
✪	✪	▣	250,000 – 1,000,000
✪	✪	•	Under 250,000

International boundary
State boundary

0   100   200   300   400 Miles
0   200   400   600 Kilometers

ICELAND
Reykjavík

FAROE ISLANDS
(Den.)

NORWEGIAN SEA

Arctic Circle

Kiruna

Hammerfes

Trondheim

Umeå

SWEDEN

NORWAY

Tamper

Bergen

Oslo

Göteborg

Stockholm

Vänern

Vättern

ATLANTIC OCEAN

SCOTLAND
Aberdeen
Glasgow
Edinburgh

UNITED

NORTHERN IRELAND
Belfast

Dublin
IRELAND
Cork

Irish Sea

KINGDOM

NORTH SEA

Skagerrak

DENMARK

Copenhagen

Kattegat

LITHUANI

Kaliningrad

RUSSA

BALTIC SEA

St. George's Channel

Liverpool
Manchester

WALES
Birmingham
Cardiff
ENGLAND

NETHERLANDS
Amsterdam
The Hague

Hamburg

Elbe

Berlin

Szczecin

Gdańsk

POLAND
Warsaw

Łódź

Plymouth

Thames
London

Antwerp
Brussels
BELGIUM

Essen
Cologne
Bonn

GERMANY

Oder

Dresden

Wrocław

Katowice

Kraków

English Channel

Strait of Dover

Le Havre

Luxembourg
LUX.

Frankfurt

Prague

CZECH REPUBLIC

Brest

Paris

Rhine

Strasbourg

Stuttgart

Danube

Munich

Vienna

SLOVAKIA

Bratislava

Nantes

Loire

Seine

FRANCE

Zurich
Bern
Geneva
SWITZERLAND

LIECH.

AUSTRIA
Graz

Budapest

HUNGARY

Bay of Biscay

A Coruña
Gijón

Bilbao

Bordeaux

Lyon

Rhône

Turin

Milan

SLOVENIA
Ljubljana

Venice

Zagreb

Genoa

Bologna

CROATIA

Belgrade

Porto

Valladolid

Toulouse

Marseille
Golfe du Lion

MONACO

Nice

Ligurian Sea

Po

SAN MARINO

Florence

BOSNIA AND HERZEGOVINA

Sarajevo

SERBIA

Split

ADRIATIC SEA

Lisbon
PORTUGAL

Tagus

Madrid

SPAIN

Ebro
Zaragoza
ANDORRA

Barcelona

Corsica

ITALY

Rome
VATICAN CITY

MONTENEGRO

Podgorica

KOSOV

Pristina

Skopje
MACE
DONIA

ALBANIA

Tiranë

Córdoba

València

Palma

Sardinia

Naples

Bari

Seville

Alacant

Strait of Gibraltar

Málaga
GIBRALTAR
(U.K.)

MEDITERRA

Cagliari

TYRRHENIAN SEA

GREEC

Algiers

Palermo

Sicily

Messina

Catania

IONIAN SEA

Pátra

MOROCCO

AFRICA

ALGERIA

TUNISIA

MALTA

NEAN SEA

30° 60° 50° 40° 30°

20° 30° 1 2 10° 3 0° 4 10° 5

10° 3 0° 4 10° 5 20°

Murmansk

WHITE SEA

Oulu

FINLAND

Arkhangel'sk

Ukhta

Severnaya Dvina

Syktyvkar

R U S S I A

Berezniki

Perm'

Helsinki

Petrozavodsk

Lake Onega

Kirov

Izhevsk

Naberezhnye Chelny

Ufa

Saint Petersburg

Cherepovets

Lake Ladoga

Rybinsk Res.

Gorki Res.

Nizhniy Novgorod

Kazan'

A S I A

Tallinn

STONIA

Lake Peipus

Tver'

Yaroslavl'

Ivanovo

Kuybyshev Res.

Rīga

LATVIA

Moscow

Ryazan'

Samara

Vicebsk

Tula

Penza

Vilnius

Oka

Minsk

Bryansk

Lipetsk

Saratov

Volgograd Res.

BELARUS

Homel'

Voronezh

Don

Volga

KAZAKHSTAN

Ural

Aral Sea

UZBEKISTAN

Chornobyl'

Kiev

Kharkiv

Volgograd

Atyraū

L'viv

Vinnytsia

UKRAINE

Dnieper

Dnipro-petrovs'k

Luhans'k

Tsymlyansk Res.

Volga

Astrakhan'

Dniester

Kryvyi Rih

Zaporizhzhia

Mariupol'

Donets'k

Rostov-na-Donu

CASPIAN SEA

TURKMENISTAN

MOLDOVA

Iaşi

Chişinău

Sea of Azov

Krasnodar

Stavropol'

Cluj-Napoca

Odesa

Vladikavkaz

ROMANIA

Galaţi

Simferopol'

Craiova

Bucharest

Constanţa

Sevastopol'

GEORGIA

Tbilisi

Baku

Danube

BULGARIA

Varna

B L A C K   S E A

AZERBAIJAN

Sofia

Plovdiv

ARMENIA

Yerevan

AZER.

Istanbul

Tehran

Thessaloniki

Sea of Marmara

Ankara

TURKEY

IRAN

AEGEAN SEA

Athens

IRAQ

SYRIA

Baghdad

Crete

CYPRUS

LEBANON

© Rand McNally
Made in U.S.A.
M-100128-3

70° 7 40° 8 50° 9 60° 10 70° 11 80°

6 30° 7 40° 8 9

Climate

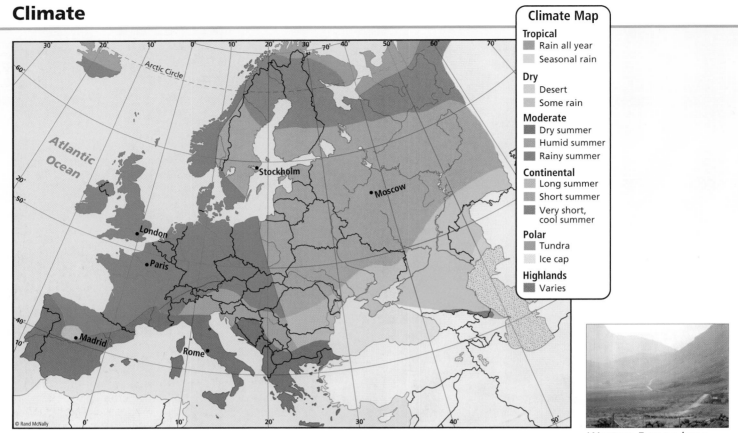

Climate Map

Tropical
- Rain all year
- Seasonal rain

Dry
- Desert
- Some rain

Moderate
- Dry summer
- Humid summer
- Rainy summer

Continental
- Long summer
- Short summer
- Very short, cool summer

Polar
- Tundra
- Ice cap

Highlands
- Varies

Western Europe has a mild, rainy climate.

Population

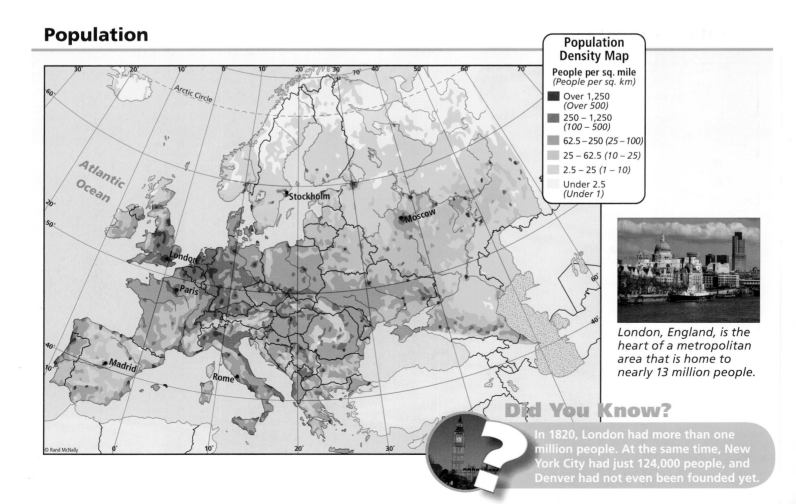

Population Density Map

People per sq. mile
(People per sq. km)

- Over 1,250 (Over 500)
- 250 – 1,250 (100 – 500)
- 62.5 – 250 (25 – 100)
- 25 – 62.5 (10 – 25)
- 2.5 – 25 (1 – 10)
- Under 2.5 (Under 1)

London, England, is the heart of a metropolitan area that is home to nearly 13 million people.

Did You Know?

In 1820, London had more than one million people. At the same time, New York City had just 124,000 people, and Denver had not even been founded yet.

Environments

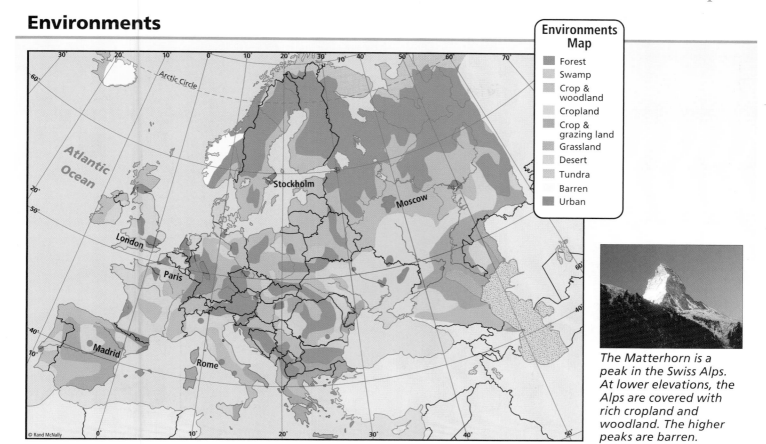

Environments Map

- ☐ Forest
- ☐ Swamp
- ☐ Crop & woodland
- ☐ Cropland
- ☐ Crop & grazing land
- ☐ Grassland
- ☐ Desert
- ☐ Tundra
- ☐ Barren
- ☐ Urban

The Matterhorn is a peak in the Swiss Alps. At lower elevations, the Alps are covered with rich cropland and woodland. The higher peaks are barren.

Economic Activities

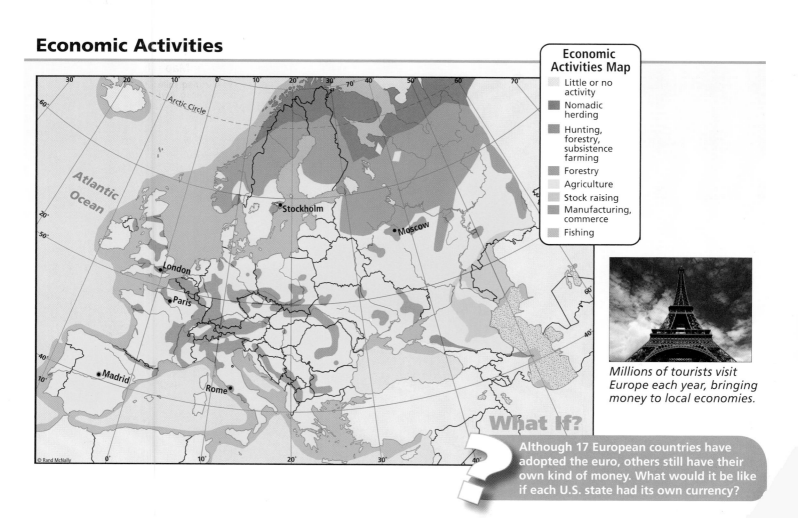

Economic Activities Map

- ☐ Little or no activity
- ☐ Nomadic herding
- ☐ Hunting, forestry, subsistence farming
- ☐ Forestry
- ☐ Agriculture
- ☐ Stock raising
- ☐ Manufacturing, commerce
- ☐ Fishing

Millions of tourists visit Europe each year, bringing money to local economies.

What If?

? Although 17 European countries have adopted the euro, others still have their own kind of money. What would it be like if each U.S. state had its own currency?

Natural Hazards

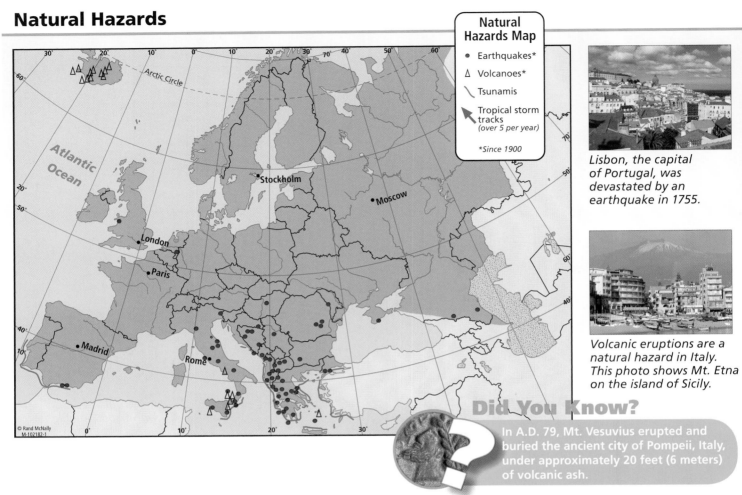

Natural Hazards Map

- Earthquakes*
- △ Volcanoes*
- \ Tsunamis
- ↖ Tropical storm tracks *(over 5 per year)*

*Since 1900

© Rand McNally
M-102182-1

Lisbon, the capital of Portugal, was devastated by an earthquake in 1755.

Volcanic eruptions are a natural hazard in Italy. This photo shows Mt. Etna on the island of Sicily.

Did You Know?

In A.D. 79, Mt. Vesuvius erupted and buried the ancient city of Pompeii, Italy, under approximately 20 feet (6 meters) of volcanic ash.

Transportation

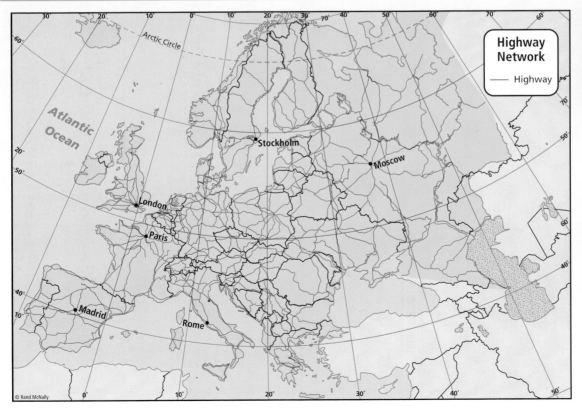

Highway Network

— Highway

© Rand McNally

A canal boat is a modern means of transportation in Amsterdam, the Netherlands.

High-speed rail systems connect many European cities.

Energy

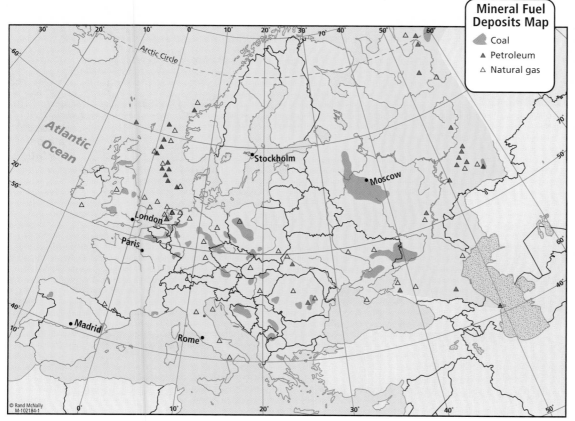

Energy Plants Map
- ■ Nuclear
- ● Hydroelectric
- ▽ Geothermal

Mineral Fuel Deposits Map
- ◗ Coal
- ▲ Petroleum
- △ Natural gas

In Iceland, water from hot springs heats homes and fuels geothermal plants.

Hydroelectric power is important in some parts of Europe. This dam is in Switzerland.

North Sea oil and gas are important sources of energy for the United Kingdom and Norway.

Coal was the first fuel for modern factories, but today it is less favored because it is so polluting.

Africa

African elephant

Africa is a huge continent. It is larger than every other continent except Asia. More than 1 billion people live in Africa, and the population is growing fast.

The Sahara, the largest desert in the world, covers most of northern Africa. South of the Sahara is the Sahel, an area of dry grasslands. The Sahel expands and recedes with changes in climate.

The tropical rain forests of central Africa provide a natural habitat for gorillas, chimpanzees, and monkeys. North and south of the rain forests and in eastern Africa are vast grassy plains, or savannas. These plains are home to herds of grazing animals, as well as elephants, lions, and other animals most of us see only in zoos.

During the late 19th and early 20th centuries, European countries occupied and governed most of Africa. Today, almost every country in Africa is independent. Africa has 54 countries, the most of any continent.

Many of Africa's people are poor, and they face great challenges in health care, literacy, and life expectancy. Terrible civil wars have torn apart several nations.

Nevertheless, Africa has many possibilities. Hydroelectric power from the Congo and other rivers, minerals such as iron and copper, and improved farming methods offer the hope of better lives to many Africans.

Did You Know?

Tectonic forces are slowly tearing Africa into two parts. The Rift Valley in eastern Africa marks the dividing line.

A Historical Look At Africa

Circa 140,000 B.C.E.

The first people live in Africa.

Circa 8000 B.C.E.

Permanent fishing communities are established along many lakes and rivers.

3000 B.C.–400 A.D.

The Nile River valley is home to thriving civilizations.

500–1076

The kingdom of Ghana flourishes in the Sahel.

African Independence

In the late 19th and early 20th centuries, European countries colonized in almost all of Africa. As recently as 1950, only four African countries were independent: Egypt, Ethiopia, Liberia, and South Africa. During the following decades, anti-colonial movements gathered strength across the continent. By the end of the 1970s, a total of 43 countries had become independent. Today, the only African country that is not independent is Western Sahara, which is under the control of Morocco.

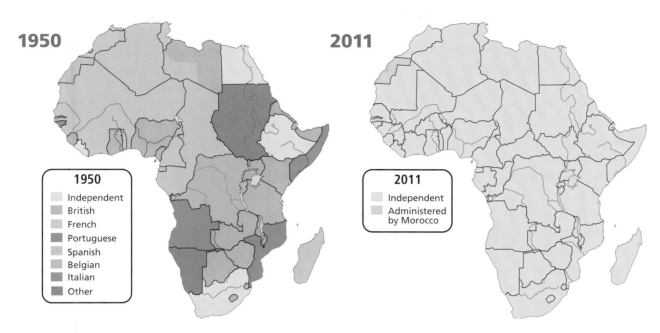

1950

1950	
	Independent
	British
	French
	Portuguese
	Spanish
	Belgian
	Italian
	Other

2011

2011	
	Independent
	Administered by Morocco

The People of Africa

There are more than 800 ethnic groups in Africa. It is estimated that the people of Africa speak between 800 and 1,600 different languages.

Children from Egypt

Girl from Ethiopia

Children from South Africa

Shepherd from the Sahel

1847
Liberia, founded as a refuge for freed slaves returning to Africa, gains independence.

1885
European countries divide Africa into colonies.

1950–1979
Most African countries become independent.

1991
South Africa ends apartheid, the official policy of racial segregation.

2011
South Sudan gains independence.

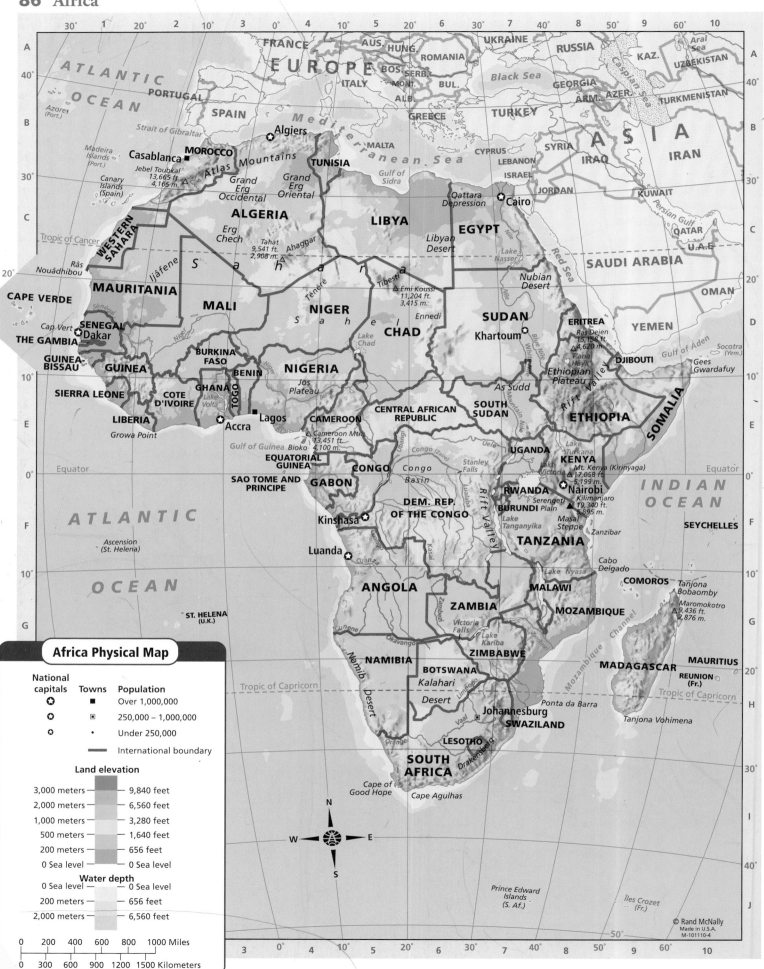

Africa Physical Map

National capitals

⊛ Over 1,000,000
⊛ 250,000 – 1,000,000
⊛ Under 250,000

Towns

■ Over 1,000,000
▣ 250,000 – 1,000,000
▪ Under 250,000

— International boundary

Land elevation

3,000 meters	9,840 feet
2,000 meters	6,560 feet
1,000 meters	3,280 feet
500 meters	1,640 feet
200 meters	656 feet
0 Sea level	0 Sea level

Water depth

0 Sea level	0 Sea level
200 meters	656 feet
2,000 meters	6,560 feet

0 200 400 600 800 1000 Miles
0 300 600 900 1200 1500 Kilometers

© Rand McNally
Made in U.S.A.
M-101110-4

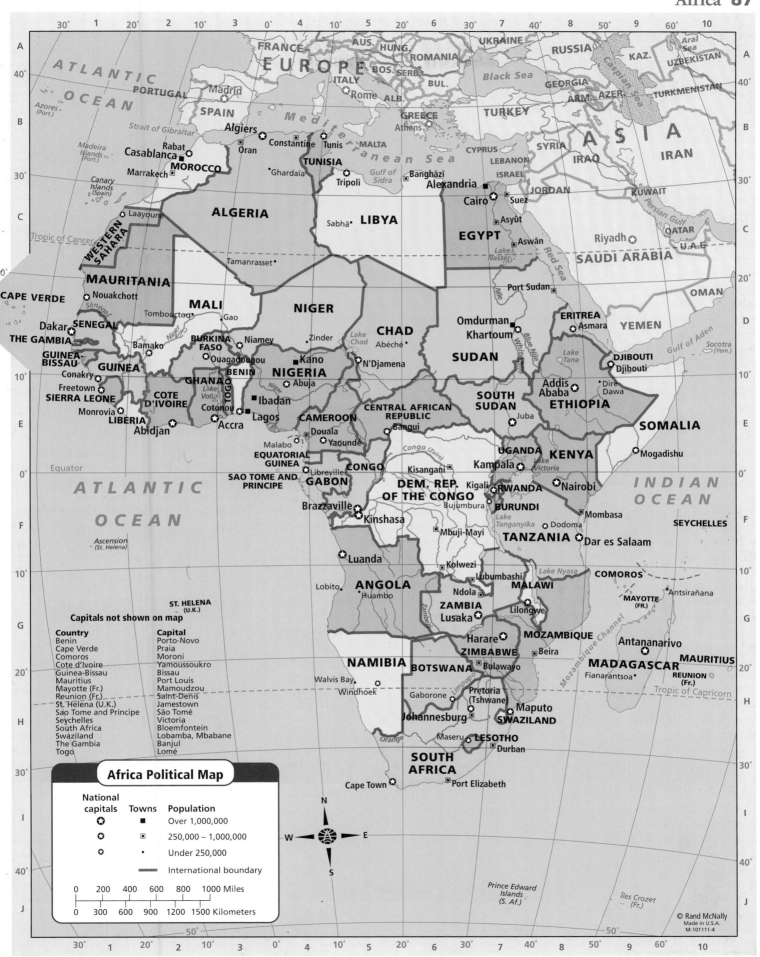

Africa Political Map

National capitals	Towns	Population
✪	■	Over 1,000,000
✪	▣	250,000 – 1,000,000
✪	•	Under 250,000
	— International boundary

0 200 400 600 800 1000 Miles
0 300 600 900 1200 1500 Kilometers

Capitals not shown on map

Country	Capital
Benin	Porto-Novo
Cape Verde	Praia
Comoros	Moroni
Cote d'Ivoire	Yamoussoukro
Guinea-Bissau	Bissau
Mauritius	Port Louis
Mayotte (Fr.)	Mamoudzou
Reunion (Fr.)	Saint-Denis
St. Helena (U.K.)	Jamestown
São Tome and Principe	São Tomé
Seychelles	Victoria
South Africa	Bloemfontein
Swaziland	Lobamba, Mbabane
The Gambia	Banjul
Togo	Lomé

© Rand McNally
Made in U.S.A.
M-101111-4

Environments

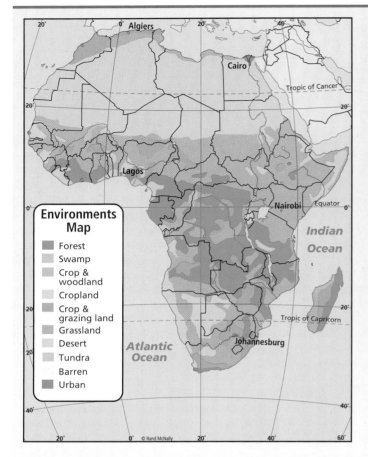

Tropical rain forests of central Africa are hot and humid. Jungles are areas of dense, tangled plant growth in these forests.

An erg is a large area of sand dunes in a desert. Deserts cover about one-third of Africa.

Savannas, areas of grassland with few trees, cover about two-fifths of Africa's land area. Similar areas in North America are called prairies.

The region known as the Sahel borders the Sahara on the south. Overfarming, overgrazing, and droughts have caused parts of the Sahel to become desert.

An oasis in a desert is found where underground water comes to the surface.

Although many Africans still live in the countryside, Africa has large, modern cities. This is a view of Johannesburg, South Africa.

Africa's most fertile cropland is found along its rivers. This farm is in Egypt's Nile River valley.

Climate

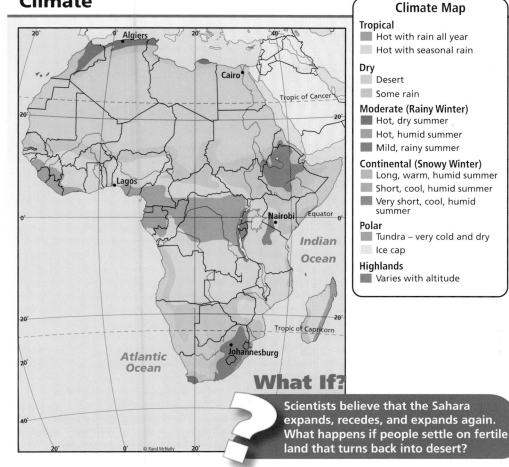

Climate Map

Tropical
- Hot with rain all year
- Hot with seasonal rain

Dry
- Desert
- Some rain

Moderate (Rainy Winter)
- Hot, dry summer
- Hot, humid summer
- Mild, rainy summer

Continental (Snowy Winter)
- Long, warm, humid summer
- Short, cool, humid summer
- Very short, cool, humid summer

Polar
- Tundra – very cold and dry
- Ice cap

Highlands
- Varies with altitude

The Sahara

The Sahara is the largest hot desert in the world. It covers about 3.3 million square miles (about 8.5 million square kilometers). The name "Sahara" comes from the Arabic word for desert.

The highest temperature ever recorded in the world was in the Sahara: 136° F (58° C). But the Sahara can be very cold at night because the dry air does not hold much heat. The daytime and nighttime temperatures can differ by as much as 100° F (56° C).

On average, rainfall in the Sahara is less than 10 inches (25 centimeters) per year. There may be no rain at all for years at a time.

Besides sand, the Sahara has vast areas of gravel, rocky plateaus, and volcanic mountains.

What If?

? Scientists believe that the Sahara expands, recedes, and expands again. What happens if people settle on fertile land that turns back into desert?

Animals of the Savanna

African elephants

Lion

Thomson's gazelles

White rhinoceroses

Cheetah and cubs

Zebras

Natural Hazards

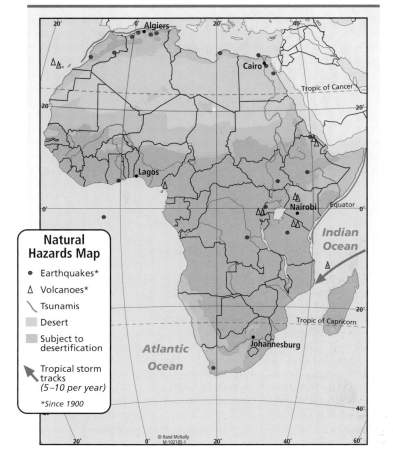

Natural Hazards Map

- • Earthquakes*
- Δ Volcanoes*
- \ Tsunamis
- Desert
- Subject to desertification
- ↖ Tropical storm tracks (5–10 per year)

*Since 1900

Population

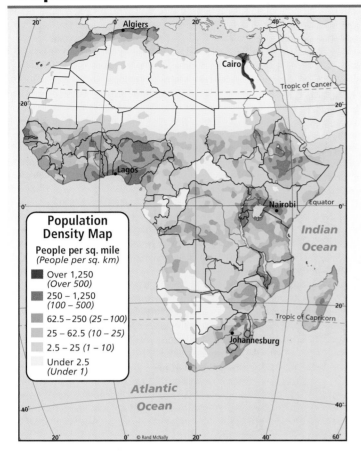

Life Expectancy

Life expectancy varies widely across Africa. In recent decades, the deadly disease AIDS has shortened the average life span of people in many African countries, especially those south of the Sahara Desert.

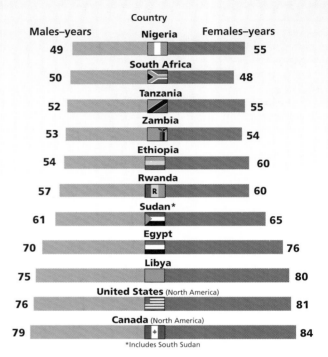

Males–years	Country	Females–years
	Nigeria	
49		55
	South Africa	
50		48
	Tanzania	
52		55
	Zambia	
53		54
	Ethiopia	
54		60
	Rwanda	
57		60
	Sudan*	
61		65
	Egypt	
70		76
	Libya	
75		80
	United States (North America)	
76		81
	Canada (North America)	
79		84

*Includes South Sudan

Transportation

Did You Know?

During the 1967 war with Israel, Egypt sank ships in the Suez Canal to block traffic. The canal stayed closed for eight years.

Fewer than 10% of the roads in Africa are paved.

Camels are still used to transport goods across the desert. Their heavy-lidded eyes and closeable nostrils offer protection in sandstorms, and they can travel long distances without water.

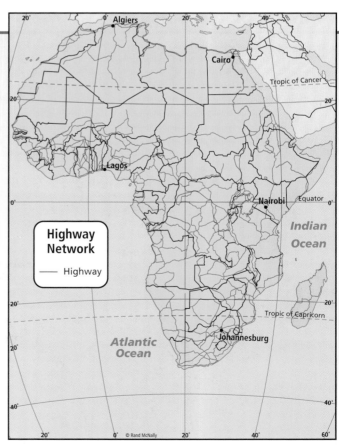

Highway Network
— Highway

Economic Activities

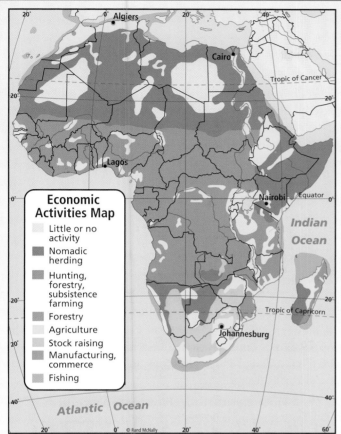

Economic Activities Map

- Little or no activity
- Nomadic herding
- Hunting, forestry, subsistence farming
- Forestry
- Agriculture
- Stock raising
- Manufacturing, commerce
- Fishing

© Rand McNally

Per Capita Income

Per capita income measures the relative wealth of countries. Most African countries have per capita incomes far below those of the three wealthy non-African countries included in this graph: Sweden, Canada, and the United States.

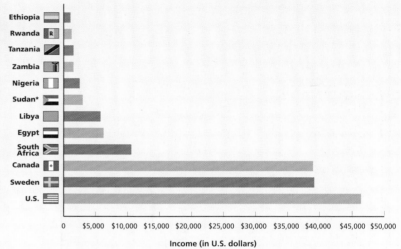

Income (in U.S. dollars)

*Includes South Sudan

In many parts of Africa, nomadic herding is the way of life for most people.

The monuments of ancient Egypt attract millions of visitors each year. Tourism revenue is an important contributor to Egypt's economy.

About 65% of all Africans make a living by farming.

World Gold Production

- South Africa 17%
- United States 13%
- Australia 11%
- China 7%
- Canada 6%
- Russia 6%
- All other countries 40%

World Platinum Production

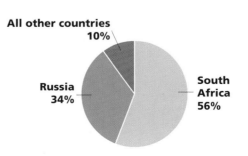

- All other countries 10%
- South Africa 56%
- Russia 34%

World Diamond Production

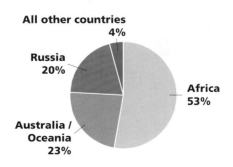

- All other countries 4%
- Africa 53%
- Australia / Oceania 23%
- Russia 20%

One reason for the high annual per capita income for South Africa is that it is rich in gold, platinum, and diamonds. Discovery of these precious mineral resources in the 1800s brought many Europeans to settle in South Africa.

Asia

Asia is the world's largest continent, and it is immense. It covers more than 17 million square miles (44 million square kilometers). It stretches from the sands of the Middle Eastern deserts in the west to the island country of Japan in the east. In the north, Siberian Russia extends beyond the Arctic Circle, while in the south Indonesia reaches the equator.

Asia is home to some of the world's oldest civilizations. Farming, cities, and writing began in Mesopotamia, in the Indus River valley, and in China thousands of years ago. Asians also invented many things that we use today, such as the idea of zero, paper, the printing press, and the magnetic compass.

Many countries in Asia are working to develop their economies, and their people still have difficult lives. Other Asian countries such as Japan, Taiwan, and Singapore are economic powers. The fortunes of the oil-rich countries of the Middle East depend on the value of their oil exports.

Asia has more people than any other continent: 4.2 billion, which is about 60% of the world's people. China alone has 1.3 billion people, and India has passed one billion. Eastern China is as densely populated as the New York City urban area.

Terraced rice field in Bali, Indonesia

Mt. Fuji in Japan

Limestone pinnacles along the Li River in China

Did You Know?

The highest point in the world (Mt. Everest) and the lowest point (the Dead Sea) are both in Asia.

A Historical Look At Asia

Circa 3500 B.C.E.

Sumerian civilization begins in Mesopotamia (modern Iraq).

A.D. 618–907

The T'ang Dynasty rules China.

Construction of the Great Wall of China begins.
403 B.C.E.

The Taj Mahal is built in India.
1631–1648

The Regions of Asia

Asia has six distinct regions. Use the political map on pages 96 and 97 to determine the countries in each region.

Central Asia
Central Asia is rugged and dry. Farming in most places is difficult, and many people make a living as nomadic herders. The region has large deposits of oil.

Southwest Asia
Most of Southwest Asia is desert and semi-desert. The region has the world's richest deposits of oil.

South Asia
India and neighboring countries make up South Asia. The Himalayas border the northeastern part of this region.

North Asia
North Asia has long, bitterly cold winters. Despite its mineral resources, fewer people live in North Asia than in any other part of the continent.

East Asia
Eastern China and its neighbors make up East Asia. About one quarter of the world's people live in East Asia.

Southeast Asia
The southeast part of the Asian mainland and many islands make up Southeast Asia. Most of the region has a tropical climate.

Central Asia

Southwest Asia

South Asia

North Asia

East Asia

Southeast Asia

1854

Japan begins trading with the United States.

Circa 1900

Britain begins developing oil fields in southwestern Iran.

1947

India is divided into two countries, India and Pakistan, and both become independent from British rule.

Powerful tsunamis devastate coastal areas of Southeast and South Asia.

2004

Mt. Everest, which rises along the border between Nepal and China, is the world's highest mountain. It is 29,028 feet (8,848 meters) high.

The Dead Sea, located between Isreal and Jordan, is the lowest point on earth. Its shore is 1,339 feet (408 meters) below sea level.

Lake Baikal in Russia is the deepest lake in the world. Its greatest depth is slightly more than a mile.

Russia's Kamchatka Peninsula is one of the most volcanically active places in the world.

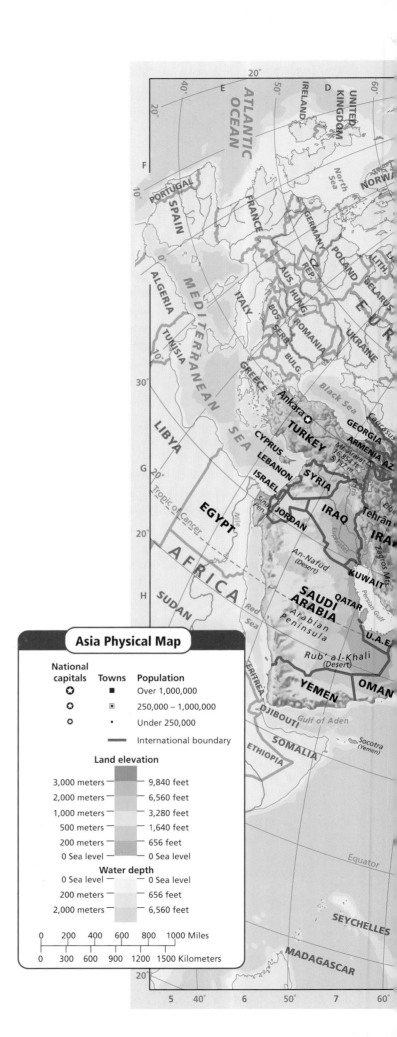

Asia Physical Map

National capitals	Towns	Population
✪	■	Over 1,000,000
✪	▣	250,000 – 1,000,000
✪	•	Under 250,000
	▬	International boundary

Land elevation

3,000 meters	9,840 feet
2,000 meters	6,560 feet
1,000 meters	3,280 feet
500 meters	1,640 feet
200 meters	656 feet
0 Sea level	0 Sea level

Water depth

0 Sea level	0 Sea level
200 meters	656 feet
2,000 meters	6,560 feet

| 0 | 200 | 400 | 600 | 800 | 1000 Miles |
| 0 | 300 | 600 | 900 | 1200 | 1500 Kilometers |

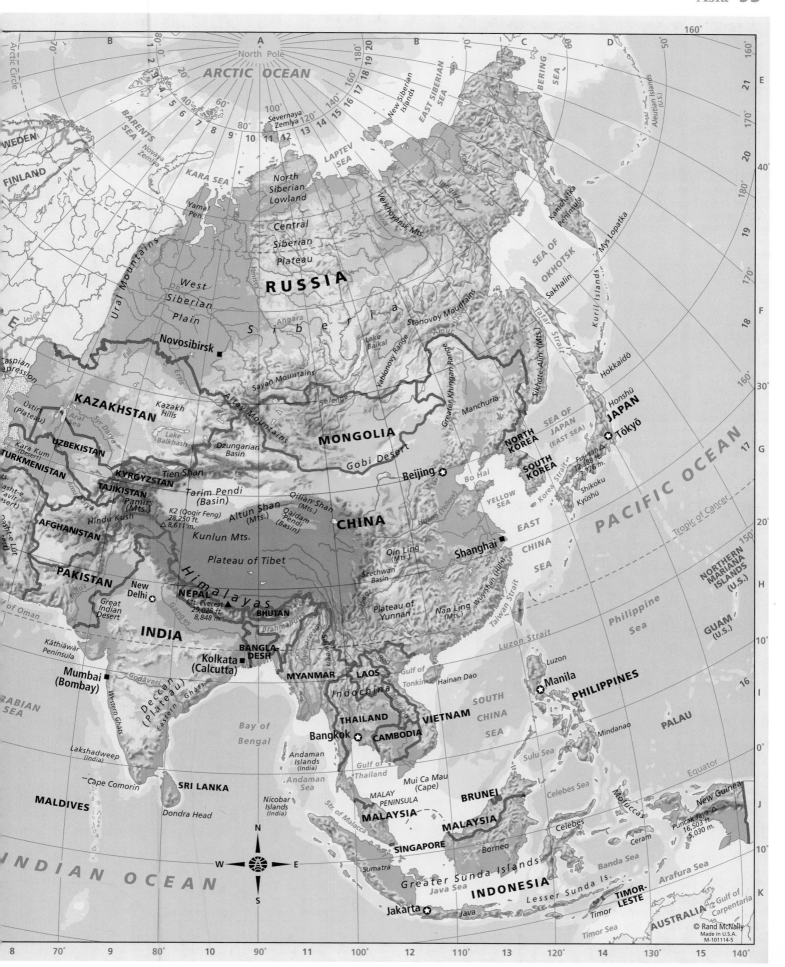

Indonesia is an island nation located in Southeast Asia. It has a larger population than all but three of the world's countries: China, India, and the United States.

China is the world's most populous country. It is home to more than 1.3 billion people.

Kyrgyzstan is located in Central Asia. It became a country when the Soviet Union broke up in 1991.

Turkey is Asia's westernmost country. Istanbul, Turkey's largest city, lies along the Bosporus Strait, which divides Asia and Europe.

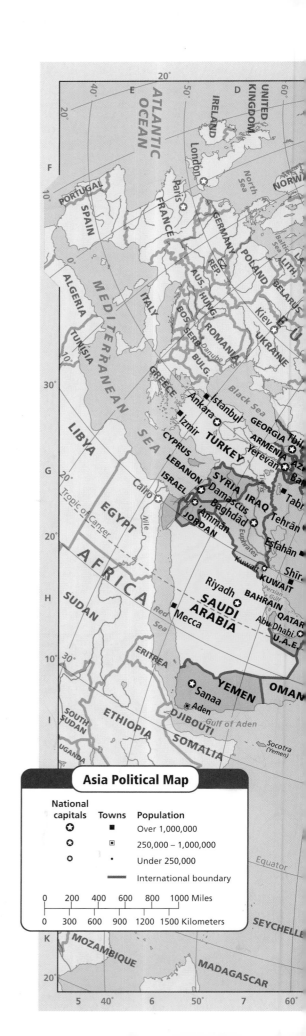

Asia Political Map

National capitals	Towns	Population
✪	■	Over 1,000,000
✪	▣	250,000 – 1,000,000
✪	•	Under 250,000
	—	International boundary

0   200   400   600   800   1000 Miles
0   300   600   900   1200   1500 Kilometers

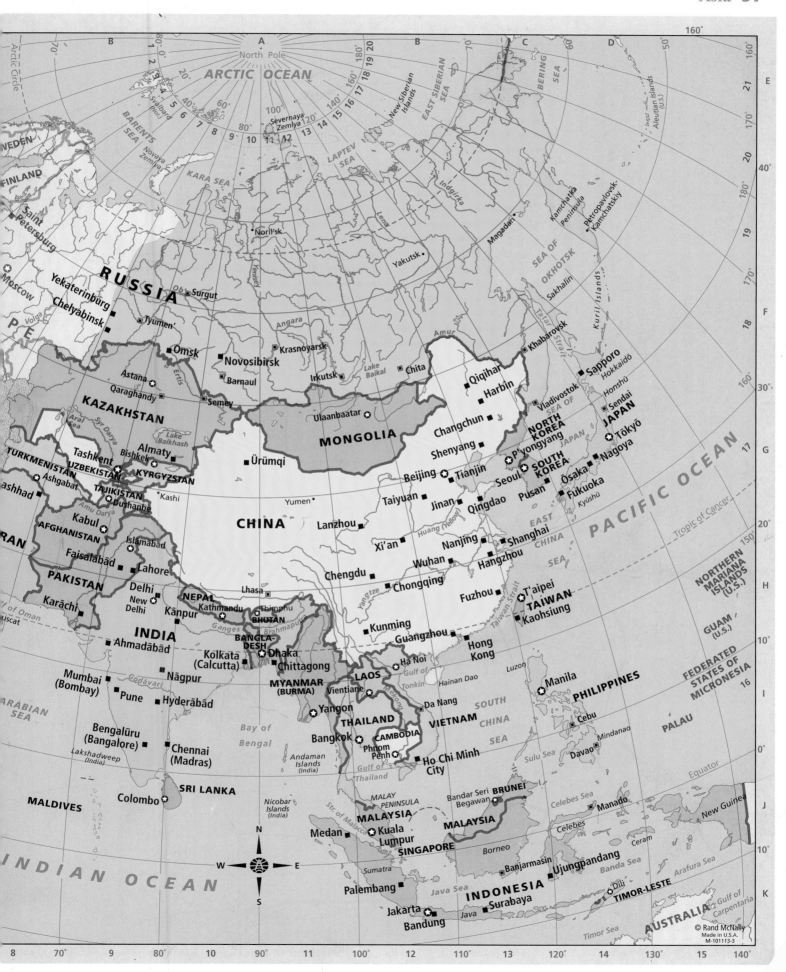

ARCTIC OCEAN

North Pole

BARENTS SEA

KARA SEA

LAPTEV SEA

EAST SIBERIAN SEA

BERING SEA

New Siberian Islands

SWEDEN

FINLAND

Saint Petersburg

Moscow

Volga

RUSSIA

Yekaterinburg

Chelyabinsk

Tyumen'

Omsk

Surgut

Krasnoyarsk

Novosibirsk

Barnaul

Irkutsk

Lake Baikal

Chita

Yakutsk

Magadan

Kamchatka Peninsula

Petropavlovsk-Kamchatskiy

Aleutian Islands (U.S.)

SEA OF OKHOTSK

Kuril Islands

Sakhalin

Tatar Strait

Khabarovsk

Noril'sk

Ob'

Yenisey

Angara

Lena

Indigirka

Amur

Astana

Qaraghandy

Semey

KAZAKHSTAN

Aral Sea

Syr Darya

Lake Balkhash

Almaty

Bishkek

Tashkent

KYRGYZSTAN

Ürümqi

Ulaanbaatar

MONGOLIA

Qiqihar

Harbin

Changchun

Shenyang

NORTH KOREA

P'yongyang

Vladivostok

SEA OF JAPAN

Sapporo

Hokkaidō

Honshū

Sendai

JAPAN

Tōkyō

Nagoya

Ōsaka

Fukuoka

Kyūshū

SOUTH KOREA

Seoul

Pusan

TURKMENISTAN

UZBEKISTAN

Ashgabat

TAJIKISTAN

Dushanbe

Kashi

Yumen

Beijing

Tianjin

Taiyuan

Jinan

Qingdao

CHINA

Lanzhou

Xi'an

Nanjing

Shanghai

EAST CHINA SEA

PACIFIC OCEAN

Tropic of Cancer

Mashhad

IRAN

Kabul

AFGHANISTAN

Faisalābād

Lahore

Islāmābād

Amu Darya

Huang (Yellow)

Chengdu

Wuhan

Chongqing

Hangzhou

Fuzhou

T'aipei

TAIWAN

Kaohsiung

Taiwan Strait

NORTHERN MARIANA ISLANDS (U.S.)

Gulf of Oman

Muscat

PAKISTAN

Karāchi

Delhi

New Delhi

Kānpur

NEPAL

Kathmandu

Thimphu

BHUTAN

Lhasa

Yangtze

Kunming

Guangzhou

Hong Kong

Ha Noi

Gulf of Tonkin

Hainan Dao

Luzon

Manila

PHILIPPINES

GUAM (U.S.)

FEDERATED STATES OF MICRONESIA

Ganges

Brahmaputra

BANGLA-DESH

Dhaka

Chittagong

MYANMAR (BURMA)

Vientiane

LAOS

VIETNAM

Da Nang

SOUTH CHINA SEA

Cebu

PALAU

INDIA

Ahmadābād

Kolkata (Calcutta)

Nāgpur

Godāvari

Mumbai (Bombay)

Pune

Hyderābād

Yangon

THAILAND

Bangkok

Mekong

Phnom Penh

CAMBODIA

Ho Chi Minh City

Mindanao

Davao

Sulu Sea

Bengalūru (Bangalore)

Chennai (Madras)

Lakshadweep (India)

ARABIAN SEA

Bay of Bengal

Andaman Islands (India)

Gulf of Thailand

Bandar Seri Begawan

BRUNEI

Celebes Sea

Manado

MALDIVES

Colombo

SRI LANKA

Nicobar Islands (India)

Str. of Malacca

MALAY PENINSULA

MALAYSIA

Celebes

Ceram

New Guinea

INDIAN OCEAN

N

W E

S

Medan

Kuala Lumpur

SINGAPORE

MALAYSIA

Borneo

Banjarmasin

Ujungpandang

Banda Sea

Arafura Sea

Sumatra

Palembang

INDONESIA

Surabaya

Java Sea

Dili

TIMOR-LESTE

Timor Sea

Jakarta

Bandung

Java

AUSTRALIA

Gulf of Carpentaria

Equator

© Rand McNally
Made in U.S.A.
M-101113-3

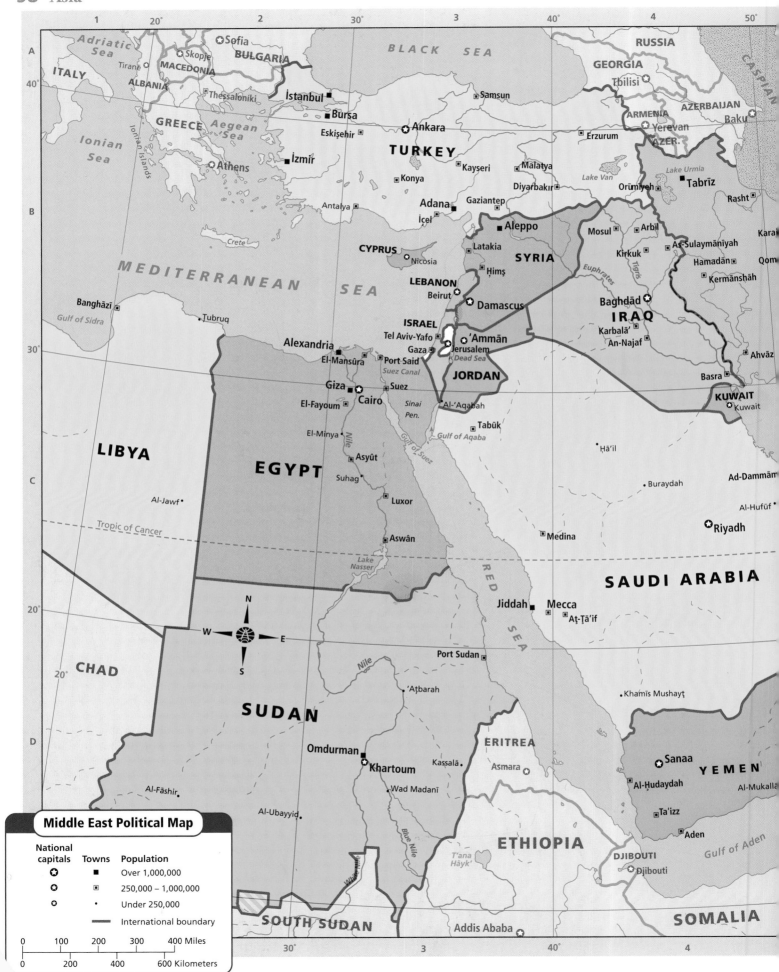

Middle East Political Map

National capitals	Towns	Population
✪	■	Over 1,000,000
◎	▫	250,000 – 1,000,000
◌	•	Under 250,000

International boundary

| 0 | 100 | 200 | 300 | 400 Miles |
| 0 | 200 | 400 | | 600 Kilometers |

The Middle East

Africa, Asia, and Europe meet in the Middle East. Since ancient times, great powerful empires have fought to control these lands, their resources, and their trade routes. Today, the oil that many Middle Eastern countries produce is valuable to rich countries. There are also deep-rooted cultural conflicts among the peoples of the region.

KAZAKHSTAN

UZBEKISTAN

TURKMENISTAN

Ashgabat

Mashhad

ehrān

IRAN

Bīrjand

AFGHAN.

Eşfahān

Yazd

Daryācheh-ye Hāmūn

Kermān

Zāhedān

Shīrāz

ūshehr

Bandar-e 'Abbās

Strait of Hormuz

ersian Gulf

HRAIN

OMAN

anama

Gulf of Oman

QATAR

Dubai

Doha

Şuḥār

Abu Dhabi

Muscat

UNITED ARAB EMIRATES

Tropic of Cancer

Şūr

OMAN

ARABIAN SEA

Şalālah

Al-Ghaydah

Socotra (Yem.)

INDIAN OCEAN

© Rand McNally
Made in U.S.A.
M-101119-2

The Middle East map (inset)

0 10 20 30 40 50 Miles
0 20 40 60 80 Kilometers

MEDITERRANEAN SEA

Ⓐ Golan Heights. Occupied and unilaterally annexed by Israel.

Ⓑ West Bank. Controlled by Israel, parts administered by the Palestinian Authority. Permanent status to be determined.

Ⓒ Gaza Strip. Administered by the Palestinian Authority following unilateral withdrawal by Israel in 2005. Permanent status to be determined.

Beirut

Sidon LEBANON

Nahr al-Līṭānī

Tyre

SYRIA

'Akko

Golan Heights Ⓐ

Sea of Galilee

Haifa

Tiberias

Nazareth

Irbid

Hadera

Janīn

Netanya

Ṭūlkarm

Jordan

Nābulus

As-Salṭ

Tel Aviv-Yafo

West Bank Ⓑ

'Ammān

Rehovot

Jericho

Ashdod

Jerusalem

Ashqelon

Bethlehem

Gaza

Hebron

Gaza Strip Ⓒ

Dead Sea

Khān Yūnis

Beersheba

Al-Karak

Port Said

Khalīg el-Tīna

El-Arish

Dimona

Suez Canal

At-Ṭafīlah

El-Qantara el-Sharqîya

ISRAEL

JORDAN

Ismailia

Negev (desert)

Great Bitter Lake

Ma'ān

EGYPT

Suez

Sinai Peninsula

Elat

Al-'Aqabah

Gulf of Suez

Gulf of Aqaba

N-CLA61400-P1- -1-1-1

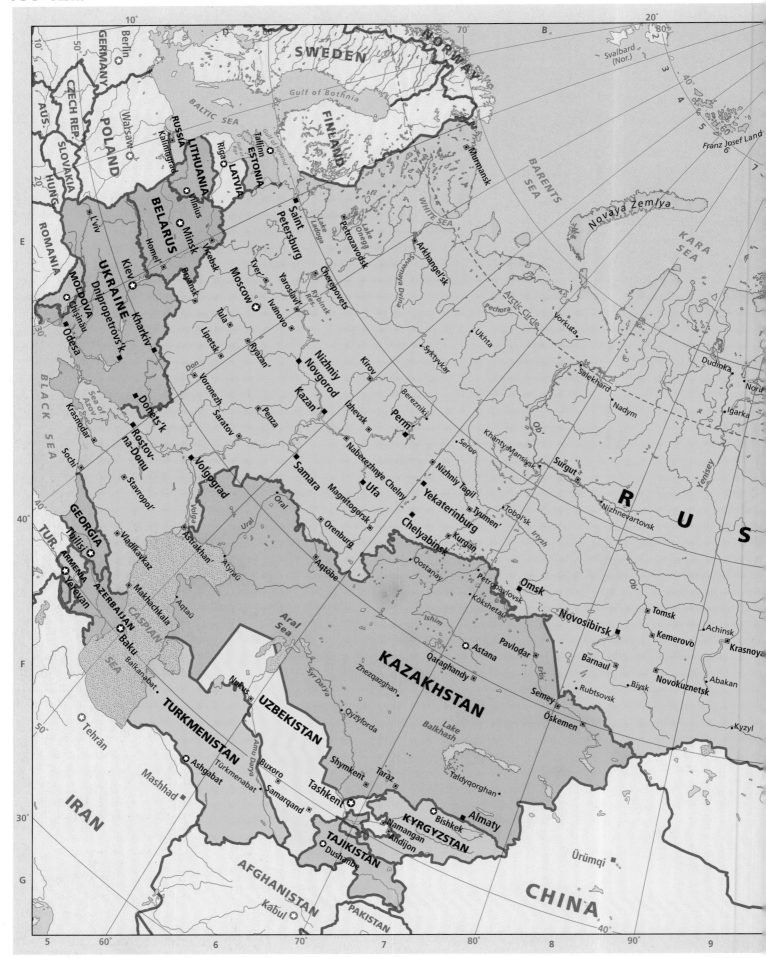

ARCTIC OCEAN

A

UNITED STATES

Bering Strait

CHUKCHI SEA

BERING SEA

Saint Lawrence Island

Wrangel Island

East Siberian Sea

Pevek

Anadyr

Arctic Circle

D

New Siberian Islands

Ostrov Novaya Sibir'

Ostrov Kotel'nyy

LAPTEV SEA

Tiksi

Indigirka

Kolyma

Ust'-Nera

Susuman

Komandorski Islands

Ust'-Kamchatsk

N
W E
S

Kamchatka Peninsula

Magadan

Petropavlovsk-Kamchatskiy

50°

Lena

Vilyuysk

Yakutsk

Nizhnyaya Tunguska

I A

Mirnyy

Aldan

Lena

Aldan

SEA OF OKHOTSK

Okha

E

Angara

Ust'-Ilimsk

Zheleznogorsk

Bratsk

Zeya

Nikolayevsk-na-Amure

Amur

Komsomol'sk-na-Amure

Sakhalin

Kuril Islands

PACIFIC OCEAN

Tatar Strait

Cheremkhovo

Lake Baikal

Chita

Amur

Svobodnyy

Blagoveshchensk

Khabarovsk

Yuzhno-Sakhalinsk

Angarsk

Irkutsk

Ulan-Ude

Birobidzhan

La Perouse Strait

Hokkaido

Sapporo

JAPAN

40°

Ulaanbaatar

Harbin

Vladivostok

Nakhodka

F

MONGOLIA

CHINA

NORTH KOREA

SEA OF JAPAN (EAST SEA)

Shenyang

P'yongyang

© Rand McNally
Made in U.S.A.
N-100133-1

Northern Eurasia Political Map

National capitals	Towns	Population
⊛	■	Over 1,000,000
⊙	▣	250,000 – 1,000,000
⊙	•	Under 250,000
	▬▬▬	International boundary

0 100 200 300 400 500 Miles

0 200 400 600 800 Kilometers

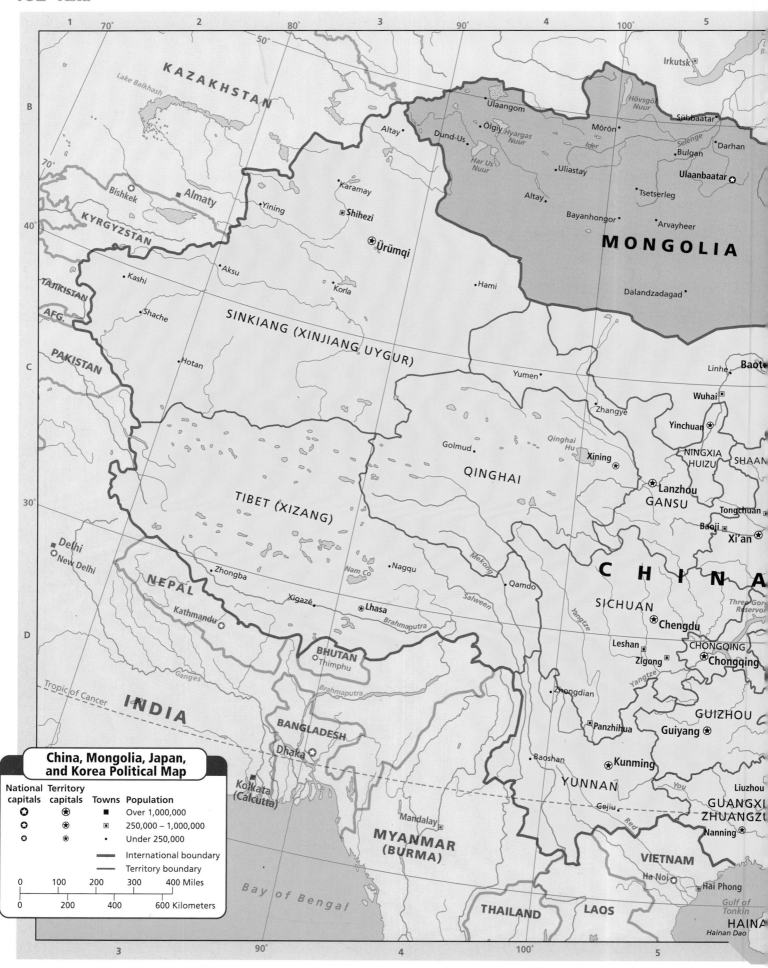

China, Mongolia, Japan, and Korea Political Map

National capitals	Territory capitals	Towns	Population
✪	✪	■	Over 1,000,000
✪	✪	▣	250,000 – 1,000,000
✪	✪	•	Under 250,000

International boundary
Territory boundary

0   100   200   300   400 Miles
0   200   400   600 Kilometers

KAZAKHSTAN
Lake Balkhash
KYRGYZSTAN
Bishkek
Almaty
TAJIKISTAN
AFG.
PAKISTAN
Yining
Kashi
Aksu
Shache
Hotan
Karamay
Shihezi
Ürümqi
Korla
SINKIANG (XINJIANG UYGUR)
Hami
Altay
Dund-Us
Ölgiy Hyargas Nuur
Har Us Nuur
Ulaangom
Mörön
Hövsgöl Nuur
Sühbaatar
Darhan
Bulgan
Ulaanbaatar
Tsetserleg
Uliastay
Altay
Bayanhongor
Arvayheer
MONGOLIA
Dalandzadagad
Irkutsk
Linhe
Baot
Wuhai
Yinchuan
NINGXIA HUIZU
SHAAN
Yumen
Zhangye
Golmud
Qinghai Hu
Xining
Lanzhou
GANSU
Tongchuan
Baoji
Xi'an
QINGHAI
TIBET (XIZANG)
Delhi
New Delhi
NEPAL
Zhongba
Nam Co
Nagqu
Qamdo
Mekong
Salween
Yangtze
Three Gor Reservoir
CHINA
SICHUAN
Chengdu
Leshan
Zigong
CHONGQING
Chongqing
Kathmandu
Xigazê
Lhasa
Brahmaputra
BHUTAN
Thimphu
Ganges
Tropic of Cancer
INDIA
BANGLADESH
Dhaka
Brahmaputra
Zhongdian
GUIZHOU
Panzhihua
Guiyang
Kolkata (Calcutta)
Baoshan
Kunming
YUNNAN
Mandalay
Liuzhou
GUANGXI ZHUANGZI
Gejiu
Nanning
Red
You
MYANMAR (BURMA)
VIETNAM
Ha Noi
Hai Phong
THAILAND
LAOS
Gulf of Tonkin
Bay of Bengal
HAINA
Hainan Dao

70°   80°   90°   100°
50°
70°
40°
30°
90°   100°

1   2   3   4   5
B
C
D

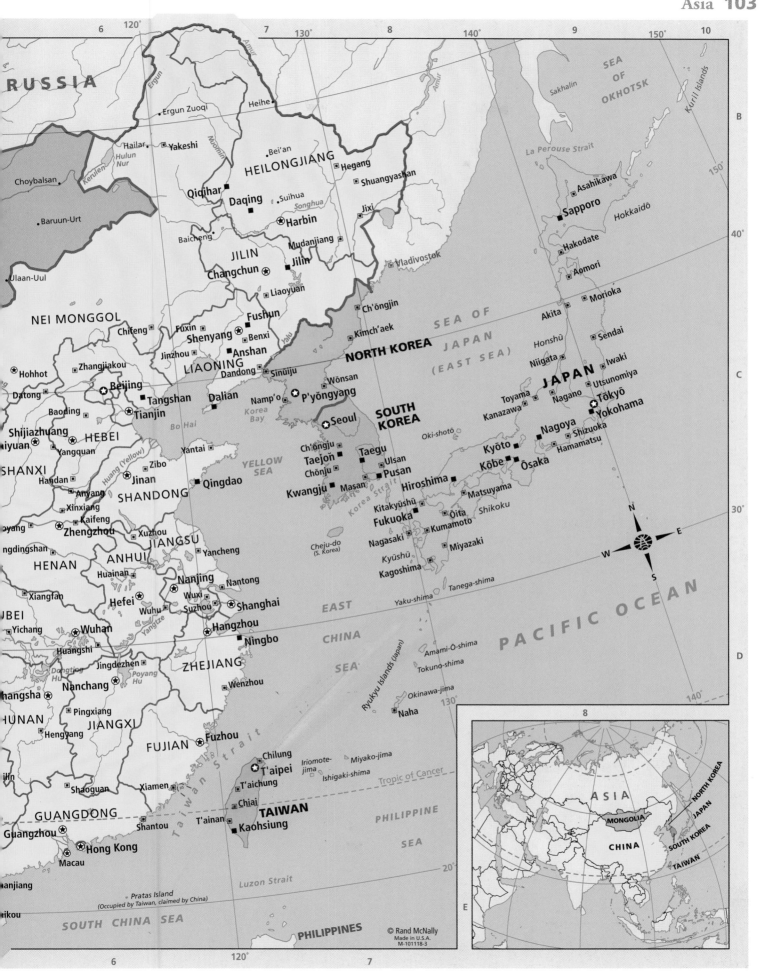

RUSSIA

6 120° 7 130° 8 140° 9 150° 10

Ergun

Amur

SEA OF
OKHOTSK

Sakhalin

Kuril Islands

B

Choybalsan

Hailar
Hulun
Nur

Yakeshi

Bei'an

HEILONGJIANG

Hegang

Shuangyashan

Heihe

Ergun Zuoqi

Nuomin

La Perouse Strait

Asahikawa

150°

Baruun-Urt

Qiqihar

Daqing

Suihua

Songhua

Jixi

Sapporo

Hokkaidō

Harbin

Baicheng

JILIN

Jilin

Mudanjiang

Vladivostok

Hakodate

40°

Ulaan-Uul

Changchun

Liaoyuan

Aomori

NEI MONGGOL

Fushun

Ch'ŏngjin

SEA OF

Morioka

Chifeng

Fuxin

Shenyang

Benxi

Kimch'aek

JAPAN

Akita

Sendai

Hohhot

Zhangjiakou

Jinzhou

Anshan

NORTH KOREA

(EAST SEA)

Honshū

Iwaki

Datong

LIAONING

Dandong

Sinŭiju

Yalu

Niigata

JAPAN

C

Beijing

Tangshan

Dalian

Namp'o

Wŏnsan

Toyama

Nagano

Utsunomiya

Baoding

Tianjin

Korea
Bay

P'yŏngyang

Kanazawa

Tōkyō

Shijiazhuang

HEBEI

Bo Hai

Seoul

SOUTH
KOREA

Oki-shotō

Nagoya

Yokohama

iyuan

Yangquan

Yantai

YELLOW

Ch'ŏngju

Kyōto

Shizuoka

SHANXI

Handan

Zibo

Jinan

SEA

Taejŏn

Taegu

Kōbe

Ōsaka

Hamamatsu

Huang (Yellow)

Chŏnju

Ulsan

Hiroshima

Anyang

Qingdao

Kwangju

Masan

Pusan

Matsuyama

Xinxiang

SHANDONG

Korea Strait

Kitakyūshū

Ōita

Shikoku

Kaifeng

Xuzhou

Fukuoka

Kumamoto

oyang

Zhengzhou

JIANGSU

Cheju-do
(S. Korea)

Nagasaki

Kyūshū

Miyazaki

ngdingshan

HENAN

ANHUI

Yancheng

Kagoshima

30°

Xiangfan

Huainan

Nanjing

Nantong

Yaku-shima

Tanega-shima

PACIFIC OCEAN

Hefei

Wuxi

Shanghai

EAST

Yangtze

Suzhou

Yichang

Wuhan

Hangzhou

CHINA

Amami-Ō-shima

Huangshi

Ningbo

SEA

Tokuno-shima

140°

hangsha

Jingdezhen

ZHEJIANG

Ryukyu Islands (Japan)

Dongting
Hu

Poyang
Hu

Okinawa-jima

130°

Nanchang

Wenzhou

D

HUNAN

Pingxiang

JIANGXI

Naha

Hengyang

FUJIAN

Fuzhou

Chilung

Iriomote-
jima

Miyako-jima

Tropic of Cancer

iHn

Shaoguan

Xiamen

T'aipei

Ishigaki-shima

T'aichung

PHILIPPINE

GUANGDONG

Shantou

Chiai

TAIWAN

Taiwan Strait

T'ainan

Kaohsiung

SEA

Guangzhou

Hong Kong

20°

Macau

anjiang

Luzon Strait

Pratas Island
(Occupied by Taiwan, claimed by China)

ikou

SOUTH CHINA SEA

PHILIPPINES

© Rand McNally
Made in U.S.A.
M-101118-3

E

6 120° 7

N
W — E
S

8

ASIA

NORTH KOREA

MONGOLIA

JAPAN

CHINA

SOUTH KOREA

TAIWAN

Climate

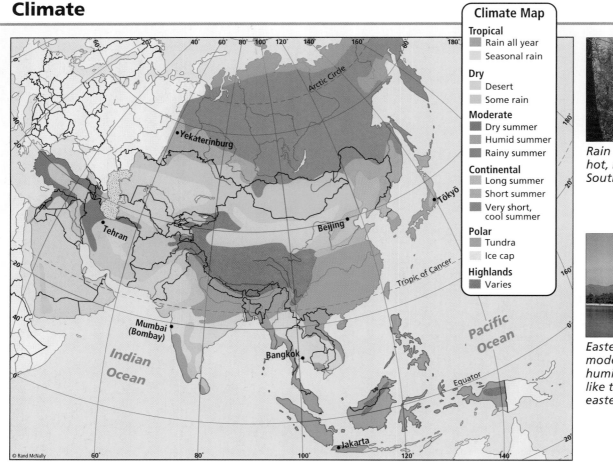

Climate Map

Tropical
- Rain all year
- Seasonal rain

Dry
- Desert
- Some rain

Moderate
- Dry summer
- Humid summer
- Rainy summer

Continental
- Long summer
- Short summer
- Very short, cool summer

Polar
- Tundra
- Ice cap

Highlands
- Varies

© Rand McNally

Rain forests thrive in the hot, rainy climate of Southeast Asia.

Eastern China has a moderate climate with humid summers. This is like the climate of the eastern United States.

Economic Activities

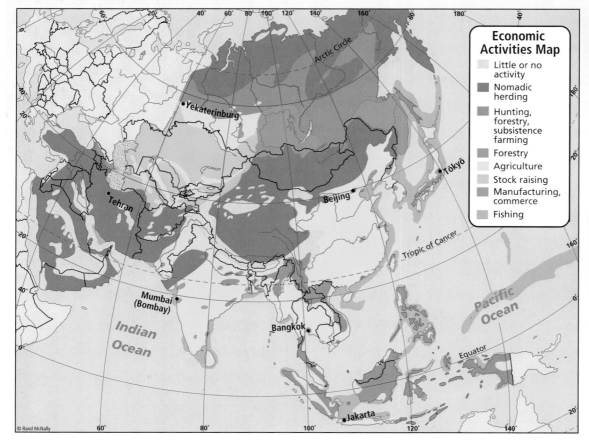

Economic Activities Map
- Little or no activity
- Nomadic herding
- Hunting, forestry, subsistence farming
- Forestry
- Agriculture
- Stock raising
- Manufacturing, commerce
- Fishing

© Rand McNally

Rice is the most important food crop in Southeast Asia.

Japan sends many of its exports to the United States, but it trades with other countries, too. Trading with many countries helps a country continue to earn money if one trading partner has economic problems.

Populations

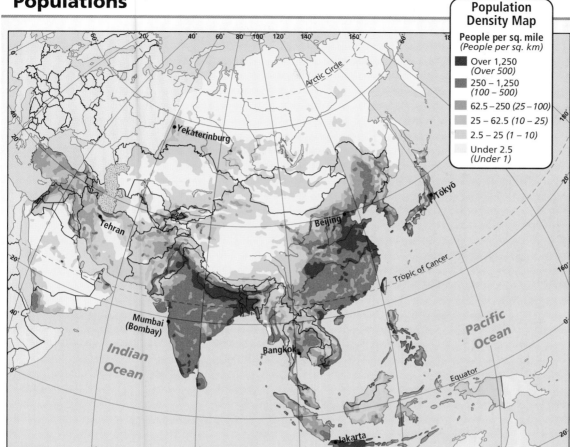

Population Density Map

People per sq. mile
(People per sq. km)

- Over 1,250 *(Over 500)*
- 250 – 1,250 *(100 – 500)*
- 62.5 – 250 *(25 – 100)*
- 25 – 62.5 *(10 – 25)*
- 2.5 – 25 *(1 – 10)*
- Under 2.5 *(Under 1)*

Seoul, South Korea, is home to more than 9.7 million people.

Bangladesh is one of the most densely populated countries in the world.

Much of Mongolia is sparsely populated.

India and China

China and India are the world's population giants. Both have populations of more than one billion people. India's population, however, is growing faster. By 2040 it will be larger than China's. Since about 1980, China has brought down its rate of population growth by strictly limiting how many children a family may have.

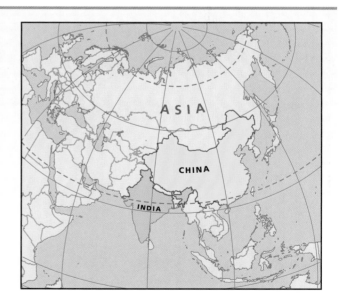

India and China Population Growth

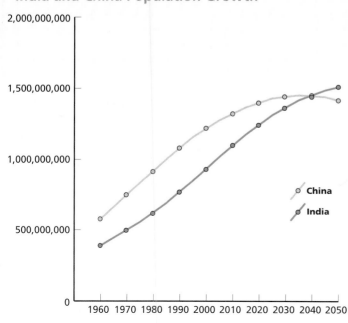

- ○ China
- ／ India

What If?

? What do you think life in India will be like if the population continues to grow rapidly?

Transportation

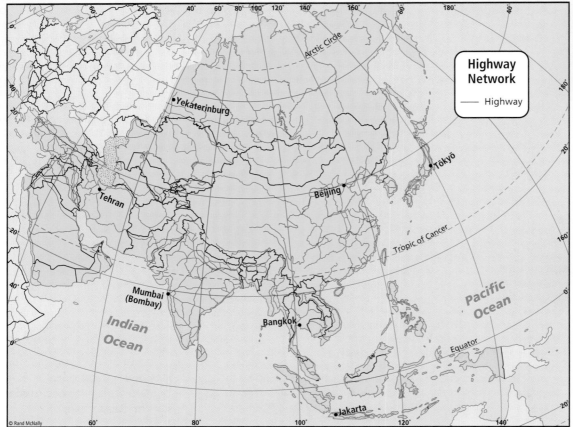

Highway Network
— Highway

Japan's bullet trains can travel at speeds of up to 155 miles per hour (249 kilometers per hour).

Mountainous terrain makes road-building difficult in many parts of Asia.

Environments

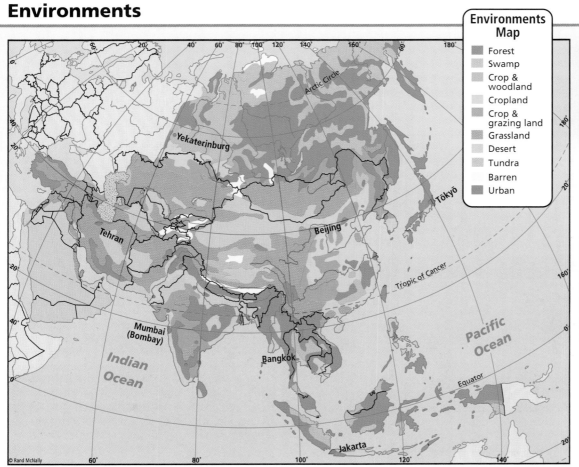

Environments Map
- Forest
- Swamp
- Crop & woodland
- Cropland
- Crop & grazing land
- Grassland
- Desert
- Tundra
- Barren
- Urban

The country of Nepal lies along the southern edge of the Himalayas. Thick woodlands cover some of the lower elevations.

Grasslands called steppes cover much of Central Asia. This photo shows camels on a steppe in Mongolia.

Natural Hazards

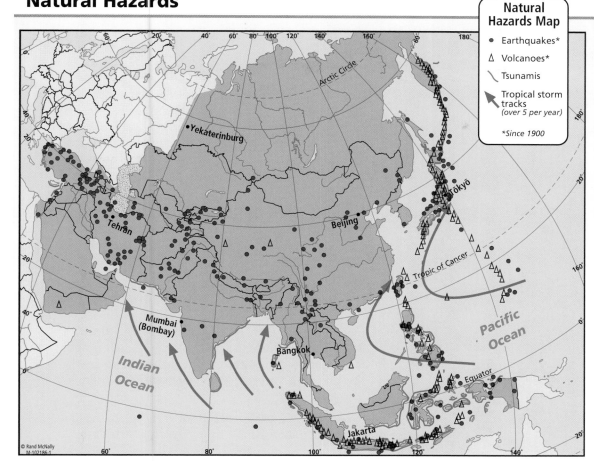

Tsunamis

Tsunamis are huge ocean waves caused by underwater earthquakes or volcanoes. They usually travel at speeds of about 300 miles per hour (500 km/hr).

Tsunamis that reach the shore can cause terrible damage to coastal areas. On December 26, 2004, a strong earthquake off the coast of Sumatra in Indonesia caused a tsunami that destroyed huge coastal areas in Indonesia, Thailand, India, and Sri Lanka and also hit Madagascar and continental Africa. More than 200,000 people were killed. Most other tsunamis have occurred in the Pacific Ocean.

Energy

On the Mineral Fuel Deposits map, note the cluster of symbols indicating petroleum deposits around the Persian Gulf, which is near the left edge of the map. This area is part of the Middle East, which produces one-third of the world's oil.

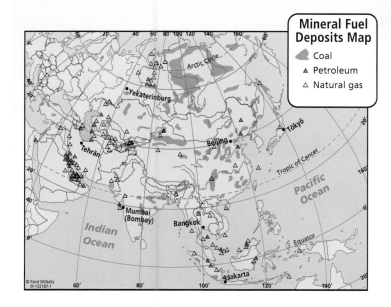

Oil exporting has brought great wealth to the countries in the Persian Gulf region of the Middle East. This photo shows an oil refinery in the United Arab Emirates.

A pipeline delivers oil to an oil tanker in Saudi Arabia.

China produces more than 45% of the world's coal.

Australia and Oceania

Australia is the only continent except Antarctica that lies completely in the Southern Hemisphere. Oceania consists of New Zealand, part of the island of New Guinea, and thousands of other islands in the Pacific Ocean. Many of these islands are tiny coral atolls where no one lives. Others are the tops of volcanoes.

Australia is the smallest continent. It is about the size of the conterminous 48 U.S. states. It has a drier climate than every other continent except Antarctica. Because Australia is in the Southern Hemisphere, it is warmer in the north than in the south.

Australia's vast, dry interior is called the Outback. Few people live there. Much of the land is used for grazing cattle and sheep on huge ranches called "stations." For many years, children on stations have "gone to school" by two-way radio connection with their teachers and other students called the School of the Air. Today, computers also provide connections for such children.

Australia's first people are the Aborigines. They came to Australia from Asia thousands of years before the first Europeans came. People from Asia also settled other islands of Oceania. New Zealand was the last place they reached. English people started coming to Australia and New Zealand in the late 1700s. People from the British Isles still make up most of the population, but Asians and people from the Pacific Islands have joined them. In both Australia and New Zealand, most people live along the coasts in modern cities.

Uluru, also known as Ayers Rock, in central Australia

Sydney, Australia

A dairy farm on New Zealand's South Island

A Historical Look At Australia

Circa 40,000 B.C.E.–30,000 B.C.E.

Aborigines arrive in Australia from Asia.

1788

The British establish the first Australian penal colony in Sydney.

1800s

Chinese settlers arrive in Northern Territory

Gold is discovered in New South Wales and Victoria.

1851

Australia's Extremes

Landforms Map
- Mountains
- Plains
- Hills and low tablelands

Indian Ocean

Gulf of Carpentaria

Cape York Peninsula

Coral Sea

Arnhem Land

Kimberley Plateau

Barkly Tableland

GREAT DIVIDING RANGE

MACDONNELL RANGES

Great Sandy Desert

Simpson Desert

Gibson Desert

Great Artesian Basin

Great Victoria Desert

Darling

Great Australian Bight

Murray

Tasman Sea

TASMANIA

© Rand McNally

Wettest place:
Bellenden Ker, Queensland 340 inches (863.6 cm) of precipitation a year

Longest coral reef:
Great Barrier Reef, northeast coast of Queensland 1,250 miles (2,000 km)

Highest point:
Mt. Kosciuszko, New South Wales 7,313 feet (2,229 m)

Coldest recorded temperature:
Charlotte Pass, New South Wales -9.4° F (-23° C)

Largest island:
Tasmania 26,400 square miles (68,400 square km)

Hottest recorded temperature:
Cloncurry, Queensland 128° F (53° C)

Largest freestanding monolith:
Uluru (Ayers Rock), Northern Territory 1,141.7 feet (348 m) high above ground by 2.2 miles (3.6 km) long by 1.5 miles (2.4 km) wide

Lowest point:
Lake Eyre, South Australia 52 feet (16 m) below sea level

Driest place:
Mulka, South Australia 4.05 inches (10 cm)/year

Longest river:
Murray River, southeastern Australia 1,558 miles (2,508 km)

Koala

Wallabies

Tasmanian devil

Wombat

1893

New Zealand is the first country to give women the right to vote.

Australia becomes a self-governing dominion within the British Empire.

1901

1976

The First Aboriginal Land Rights Act is passed.

Sydney hosts the summer Olympic Games.

2000

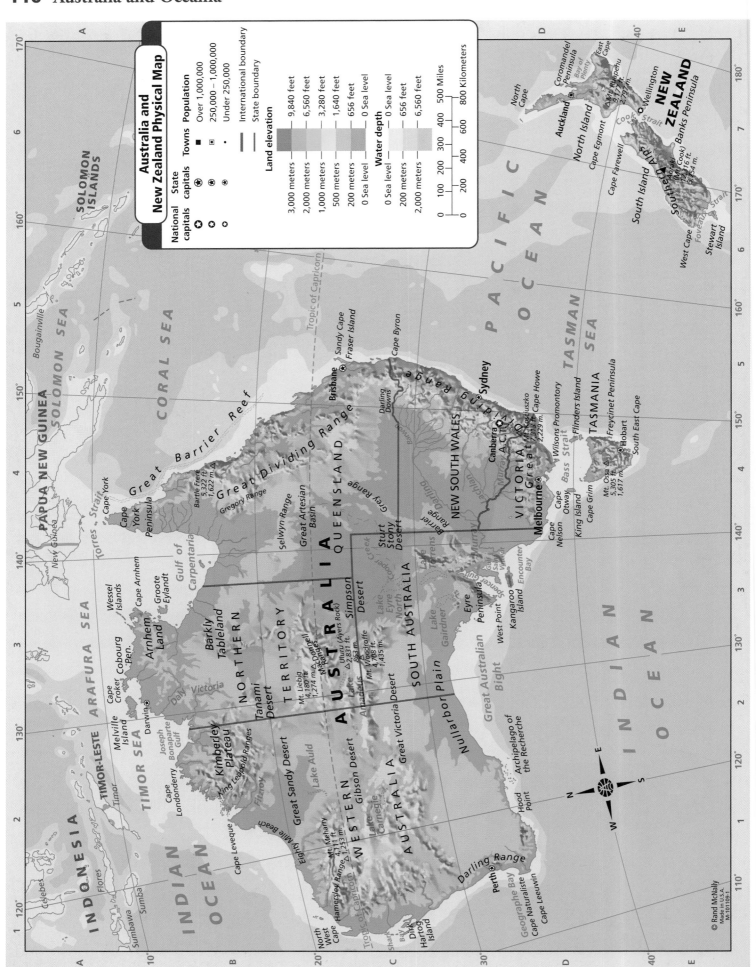

Australia and
New Zealand Physical Map

National   State   Towns Population
capitals   capitals   ◉ Over 1,000,000
⊕   ⊗   ◉ ■ 250,000 – 1,000,000
⊕   ⊗   ◉ □ Under 250,000
⊕   ⊗   •
                          International boundary
                          State boundary

Land elevation
3,000 meters   9,840 feet
2,000 meters   6,560 feet
1,000 meters   3,280 feet
500 meters   1,640 feet
200 meters   656 feet
0 Sea level   0 Sea level
Water depth
0 Sea level   0 Sea level
656 feet   200 meters
6,560 feet   2,000 meters

0   100 200 300 400 500 Miles
0   200 400 600 800 Kilometers

INDONESIA

PAPUA NEW GUINEA

SOLOMON ISLANDS

SOLOMON SEA

CORAL SEA

ARAFURA SEA

TIMOR-LESTE

TIMOR SEA

INDIAN OCEAN

Great Barrier Reef

Torres Strait

Cape York Peninsula

Gulf of Carpentaria

NORTHERN TERRITORY

Arnhem Land

Barkly Tableland

Kimberley Plateau

Tanami Desert

Great Sandy Desert

WESTERN AUSTRALIA

Gibson Desert

Great Victoria Desert

AUSTRALIA

QUEENSLAND

Great Dividing Range

Simpson Desert

Macdonnell Ranges

Uluru (Ayers Rock) △2,831 ft.
863 m.

SOUTH AUSTRALIA

Lake Eyre

Nullarbor Plain

Great Australian Bight

Darling Range

Perth ⊗

Tropic of Capricorn

NEW SOUTH WALES

Brisbane ◉
Sandy Cape
Fraser Island

Cape Byron

Sydney ⊗

Canberra ◉
A.C.T.

VICTORIA

Melbourne ⊗

Mt. Kosciuszko 7,313 ft.
2,229 m.

Cape Howe

TASMAN SEA

Bass Strait

Flinders Island

TASMANIA

Freycinet Peninsula

Hobart ⊗
South East Cape

Mt. Ossa 5,305 ft.
1,617 m.

PACIFIC OCEAN

NEW ZEALAND

North Cape

Auckland ⊗
North Island

Cape Egmont

Mt. Ruapehu 9,177 ft.
2,797 m.

Wellington ⊗
Cook Strait

Cape Farewell

South Island

Southern Alps

Mt. Tasman 11,316 ft.
Mt. Cook 12,316 ft.
3,754 m.

Banks Peninsula

West Cape

Stewart Island

Foveaux Strait

© Rand McNally
Made in U.S.A.
M-101109-1

Australia and New Zealand Political Map

Towns Population
- ■ Over 1,000,000
- ▣ 250,000 – 1,000,000
- • Under 250,000

International boundary
State boundary

	National capitals	State capitals
	⊛	⊛
	⊕	⊕
	⊙	⊙

500 Miles
800 Kilometers
0 100 200 300 400
0 200 400 600

INDONESIA

Celebes
Flores
Sumbawa
Sumba
Timor
TIMOR-LESTE

PAPUA NEW GUINEA
New Guinea
Port Moresby
Bougainville
SOLOMON ISLANDS
Honiara
VANUATU
Port Vila

SOLOMON SEA
CORAL SEA
ARAFURA SEA
TIMOR SEA
Joseph Bonaparte Gulf

Tropic of Capricorn

INDIAN OCEAN

Darwin
Katherine
Daly
NORTHERN TERRITORY
Tennant Creek
Alice Springs
Lake Amadeus

Groote Eylandt
Gulf of Carpentaria
Torres Strait
Cape York Peninsula
Weipa
Normanton
Mount Isa

QUEENSLAND
Longreach
Emerald
Charleville
Toowoomba

Cairns
Halifax Bay
Townsville
Mackay
Rockhampton
Bundaberg
Fraser Island

Brisbane
Southport

Coffs Harbour
Taree
Newcastle

NEW SOUTH WALES
Bourke
Dubbo
Broken Hill
Penrith
Sydney
Wollongong
Wagga Wagga
A.C.T.
Canberra
Albury

Darling

WESTERN AUSTRALIA
Broome
Port Hedland
Karratha
Newman
Exmouth
Carnarvon
Shark Bay
Dirk Hartog Island
Meekatharra
Lake Carnegie
Kalgoorlie-Boulder
Esperance
Archipelago of the Recherche

Geraldton
Geographe Bay
Bunbury
Albany
Perth
Derby
Fitzroy

Tropic of Capricorn

SOUTH AUSTRALIA
Lake Eyre North
Lake Torrens
Lake Gairdner
Cooper Creek
Port Augusta
Whyalla
Spencer Gulf
Kangaroo Island
Adelaide
Murray
Lachlan
Mildura
Mount Gambier
Encounter Bay
Great Australian Bight

VICTORIA
Bendigo
Ballarat
Geelong
Melbourne

King Island
Flinders Island
Bass Strait
Launceston
TASMANIA
Hobart

TASMAN SEA

PACIFIC OCEAN

Norfolk Island (Aust.)

NEW ZEALAND
North Island
Whangarei
Auckland
Hamilton
Bay of Plenty
Tauranga
Rotorua
New Plymouth
Napier
Palmerston North
Wellington
Cook Strait
Nelson
Christchurch
South Island
Timaru
Dunedin
Invercargill
Foveaux Strait
Stewart Island

INDIAN OCEAN

N E S W

© Rand McNally
Made in U.S.A.
M-100309-1

Climate

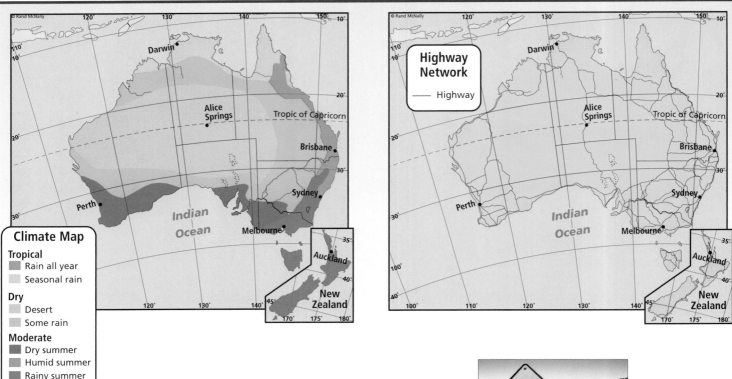

Climate Map

Tropical
- Rain all year
- Seasonal rain

Dry
- Desert
- Some rain

Moderate
- Dry summer
- Humid summer
- Rainy summer

Continental
- Long summer
- Short summer
- Very short, cool summer

Polar
- Tundra
- Ice cap

Highlands
- Varies

Transportation

Highway Network
— Highway

Did You Know?

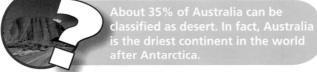

About 35% of Australia can be classified as desert. In fact, Australia is the driest continent in the world after Antarctica.

Australia's highways provide important links between widely separated towns and cities, especially in the Outback.

Environments

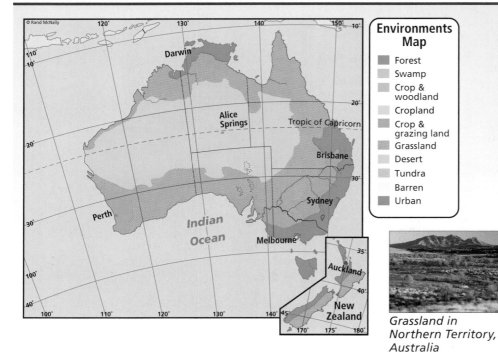

Environments Map

- Forest
- Swamp
- Crop & woodland
- Cropland
- Crop & grazing land
- Grassland
- Desert
- Tundra
- Barren
- Urban

Pinnacles Desert in Nambung National Park, Western Australia, Australia

Grassland in Northern Territory, Australia

Rain forest in Queensland, Australia

Grazing sheep, South Island, New Zealand

Economic Activities

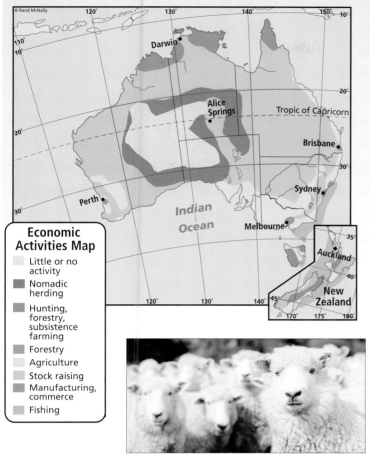

Economic Activities Map

- Little or no activity
- Nomadic herding
- Hunting, forestry, subsistence farming
- Forestry
- Agriculture
- Stock raising
- Manufacturing, commerce
- Fishing

In Australia, sheep outnumber humans four to one. In New Zealand, the ratio is seven to one. Together, the two countries produce nearly 30% of the world's wool.

Population

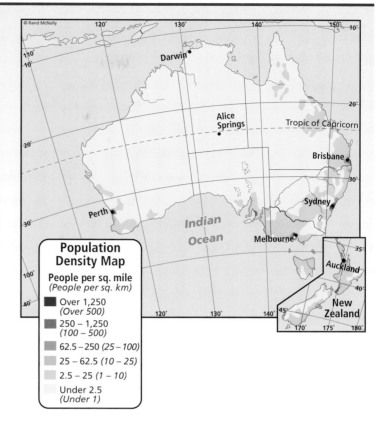

Population Density Map

People per sq. mile
(People per sq. km)

- Over 1,250 (Over 500)
- 250 – 1,250 (100 – 500)
- 62.5 – 250 (25 – 100)
- 25 – 62.5 (10 – 25)
- 2.5 – 25 (1 – 10)
- Under 2.5 (Under 1)

What If?

If all of Australia received plenty of rain, how might the population distribution be different?

The Great Barrier Reef

The Great Barrier Reef stretches for roughly 1,429 miles (2,300 km) along the northeast coast of Queensland, Australia. It is made up of more than 3,000 separate coral reefs. Together, they cover 132,974 square miles (344,400 square kilometers). The Great Barrier Reef is the largest group of coral reefs and islands in the world.

Scientists believe that the reef began forming millions of years ago. More than 600 types of soft and hard corals, in a great variety of colors, form the reef. In addition, about 1,500 species of fish live in the warm waters around the reef. Scientists warn that some human activities are causing serious damage to the reef.

More than 600 islands are found along the Great Barrier Reef. Some of them have been developed as tourist resorts, but many are uninhabited.

Green turtle

A whale shark

Acropora plate coral

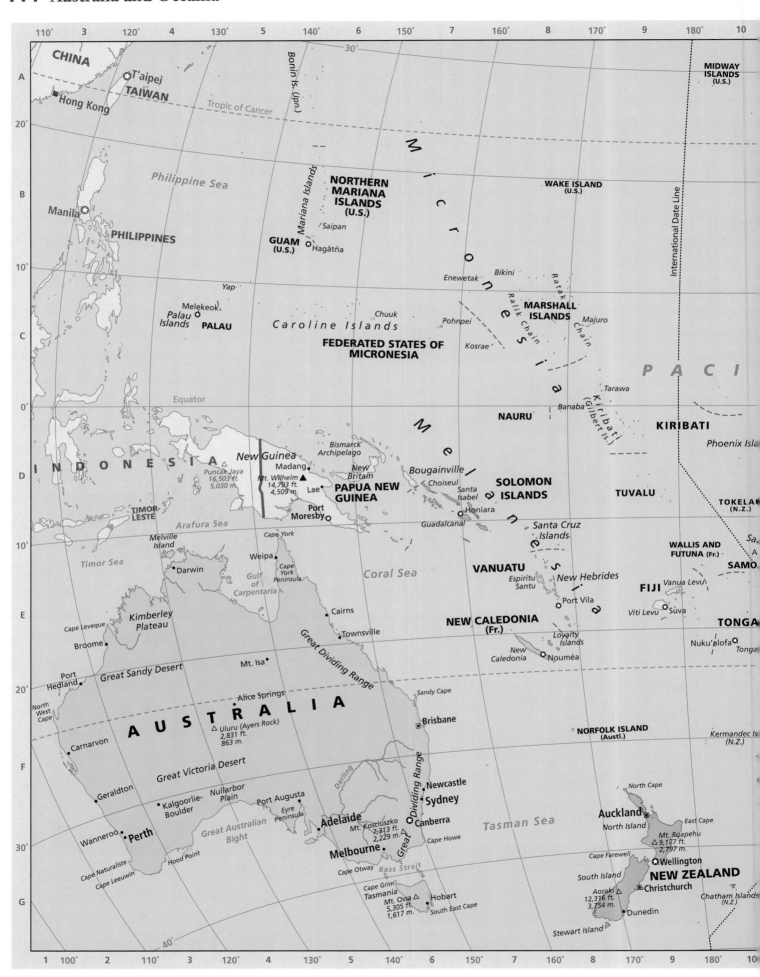

CHINA
T'aipei
TAIWAN
Hong Kong
Tropic of Cancer
Bonin Is. (Jpn.)
MIDWAY ISLANDS (U.S.)

Philippine Sea
Micronesia
NORTHERN MARIANA ISLANDS (U.S.)
Mariana Islands
WAKE ISLAND (U.S.)

Manila
PHILIPPINES
Saipan
GUAM (U.S.)
Hagåtña
Enewetak
Bikini
Ratak Chain
MARSHALL ISLANDS

Yap
Melekeok
Palau Islands
PALAU
Caroline Islands
Chuuk
Pohnpei
Kosrae
Ralik Chain
Majuro

FEDERATED STATES OF MICRONESIA

PACI

Equator
Tarawa
Banaba
Kiribati (Gilbert Is.)

NAURU
KIRIBATI
Phoenix Isla

INDONESIA
New Guinea
Madang
Bismarck Archipelago
New Britain
Bougainville
Choiseul
Santa Isabel
SOLOMON ISLANDS
TUVALU
TOKELAU (N.Z.)

Puncak Jaya 16,503 ft. 5,030 m.
Mt. Wilhelm 14,793 ft. 4,509 m.
Lae
PAPUA NEW GUINEA
Port Moresby
Honiara
Guadalcanal

TIMOR-LESTE
Arafura Sea
Santa Cruz Islands
WALLIS AND FUTUNA (Fr.)
SAMO

Melville Island
Cape York
VANUATU
Espiritu Santu
New Hebrides
FIJI
Vanua Levu

Timor Sea
Darwin
Weipa
Cape York Peninsula
Coral Sea
Port Vila
Viti Levu
Suva

Gulf of Carpentaria
NEW CALEDONIA (Fr.)
TONGA

Kimberley Plateau
Cape Leveque
Broome
Cairns
Townsville
Great Dividing Range
Loyalty Islands
New Caledonia
Nouméa
Nuku'alofa
Tonga

Port Hedland
Great Sandy Desert
Mt. Isa
North West Cape
Alice Springs
AUSTRALIA
Sandy Cape
Brisbane
NORFOLK ISLAND (Austl.)
Kermadec Is. (N.Z.)

Carnarvon
Uluru (Ayers Rock) 2,831 ft. 863 m.

Great Victoria Desert
Great Dividing Range
Newcastle
Sydney

Geraldton
Kalgoorlie-Boulder
Nullarbor Plain
Port Augusta
Eyre Peninsula
Darling
North Cape
Auckland
North Island
East Cape

Wanneroo
Perth
Great Australian Bight
Adelaide
Mt. Kosciuszko 7,313 ft. 2,229 m.
Canberra
Cape Howe
Tasman Sea
Mt. Ruapehu 9,177 ft. 2,797 m.

Cape Naturaliste
Hood Point
Melbourne
Great
Cape Otway
Bass Strait
Cape Farewell
South Island
Wellington

Cape Leeuwin
Cape Grim
Tasmania
Mt. Ossa 5,305 ft. 1,617 m.
Hobart
South East Cape
Aoraki 12,316 ft. 3,754 m.
Christchurch
NEW ZEALAND
Chatham Islands (N.Z.)

Stewart Island
Dunedin

International Date Line

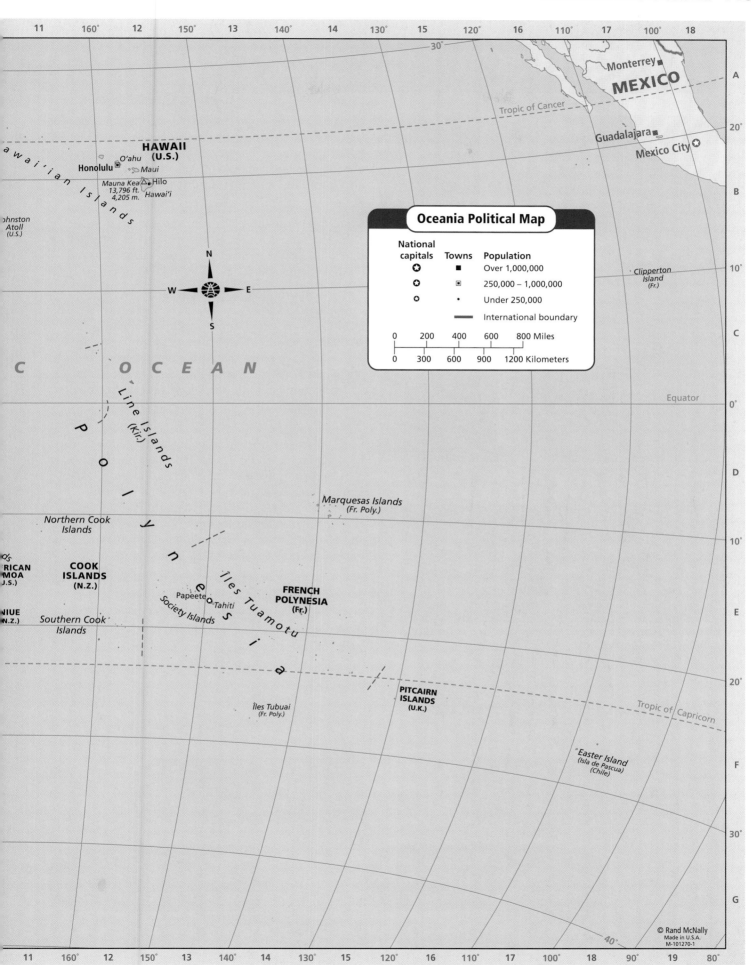

Oceania Political Map

National capitals	Towns	Population
✪	■	Over 1,000,000
✪	▣	250,000 – 1,000,000
✪	•	Under 250,000
	▬	International boundary

0   200   400   600   800 Miles
0   300   600   900   1200 Kilometers

Made in U.S.A.

MEXICO

Monterrey

Tropic of Cancer

Guadalajara

Mexico City

HAWAII (U.S.)

Honolulu   O'ahu   Maui

Mauna Kea △ Hilo
13,796 ft.   Hawai'i
4,205 m.

Hawai'ian Islands

Johnston Atoll (U.S.)

Clipperton Island (Fr.)

N
W   E
S

C   OCEAN

Equator

Line Islands (Kiri.)

Marquesas Islands (Fr. Poly.)

P O L Y N E S I A

Northern Cook Islands

COOK ISLANDS (N.Z.)

RICAN MOA U.S.)

Papeete   Tahiti

Society Islands

Îles Tuamotu

FRENCH POLYNESIA (Fr.)

NIUE (N.Z.)

Southern Cook Islands

PITCAIRN ISLANDS (U.K.)

Îles Tubuai (Fr. Poly.)

Tropic of Capricorn

Easter Island (Isla de Pascua) (Chile)

© Rand McNally
M-101270-1

Antarctica

Antarctica is the world's fifth-largest continent. Most of it lies within the Antarctic Circle. It is the world's most isolated landmass. The nearest land is the southern tip of South America, about 769 miles (more than 1,238 km) from the Antarctic Peninsula.

All the land within the Antarctic Circle has days in winter when the sun never rises and days in summer when the sun never sets. At the South Pole, between March 20 and September 21 the sun never rises, and between September 21 and March 20 it never sets.

Antarctica is the coldest place on earth. Average summer temperatures may reach only about 0° F (-18° C). Such a cold, frozen landmass produces cold winds that collide with warmer air around the coast and form a belt of storms. Antarctica receives very little precipitation. What precipitation does fall produces ice, which accumulates into thick ice sheets that gradually push toward the coast and form ice shelves over the edge of the land.

People discovered Antarctica only about 200 years ago. Exploration on land started a little more than 100 years ago. No people live on Antarctica permanently. More than a dozen countries have established scientific stations where scientists study such things as global climate change, the atmosphere's thinning ozone layer, and plant and animal life. A growing number of tourists visit the continent each year.

Scientists know that the continent has such resources as coal, but an international agreement prohibits exploiting these resources. Perhaps the most important resource is the abundant life in the cold waters off the coast.

Kayaking along the Antarctic coast

Passengers crowd the deck of an icebreaker ship as it plows through pack ice.

Explorer in a wind tunnel

A Historical Look At Antarctica

1819–1821
Fabian von Bellingshausen, a Russian, is the first European to see Antarctica.

A Norwegian expedition is the first to land on Victoria Land.
1895

1911
Roald Amundsen is the first person to reach the South Pole.

Richard Byrd flies over the South Pole.
1929

Scientific Stations in Antarctica

Frozen and isolated as it is, Antarctica offers some important advantages for researchers. Its darkness makes it a good place to study the stars. Its clean air allows studies of air quality. Scientists can see the effects of human activity. Antarctica has no borders—although seven countries have made territorial claims—so scientists from different countries can share the information they find.

A scientific station operated by Argentina

Telecommunications equipment at a scientific station

Argentina
Brazil
Chile
China
Korea
Poland
Russia
Uruguay

Palmer Station
The only U.S. station north of the Antarctic Circle

United States   Chile
Ukraine   Argentina
United Kingdom   Argentina
Argentina

Halley Station
The site of important ozone research

United Kingdom

McMurdo Station
Home to Antarctica's largest community and capable of supporting up to 1,200 people

Argentina

Germany

South Africa

United States
New Zealand

United States
South Pole   **Amundsen-Scott South Pole Station**
Located about 1,150 feet (350 m) from the geographic South Pole

India

Russia

ANTARCTICA

SANAE IV
Built on poles, since 60-80 inches (150 to 200 cm) of snow piles up in winter

Russia

Japan

France

Russia

Dumont d'Urville Station
Built in 1956 to replace a station that burned down

Vostok Station
The coldest recorded temperature on Earth, -128° F. (-89.2° C), was measured here on July 21, 1983.

China
Russia

Australia

Australia

Mawson Station
The oldest continuously inhabited station south of the Antarctic Circle

Australia

Australia

Russia

Mirny Station
Opened in 1956

Davis Station
The southernmost Australian station

Animals in Antarctica

Orcas, also known as killer whales

Wandering albatross

Emperor penguins

Leopard seal

1957–1958

The International Geophysical Year (IGY) focuses on the scientific study of Antarctica.

1991

The Protocol on Environmental Protection to the Antarctic Treaty bans commercial mining operations in Antarctica.

The Antarctic Treaty is signed. It provides for peaceful scientific cooperation in Antarctica.

1959

An iceberg 170 miles long and 25 miles wide breaks off the Ross Ice Shelf.

2000

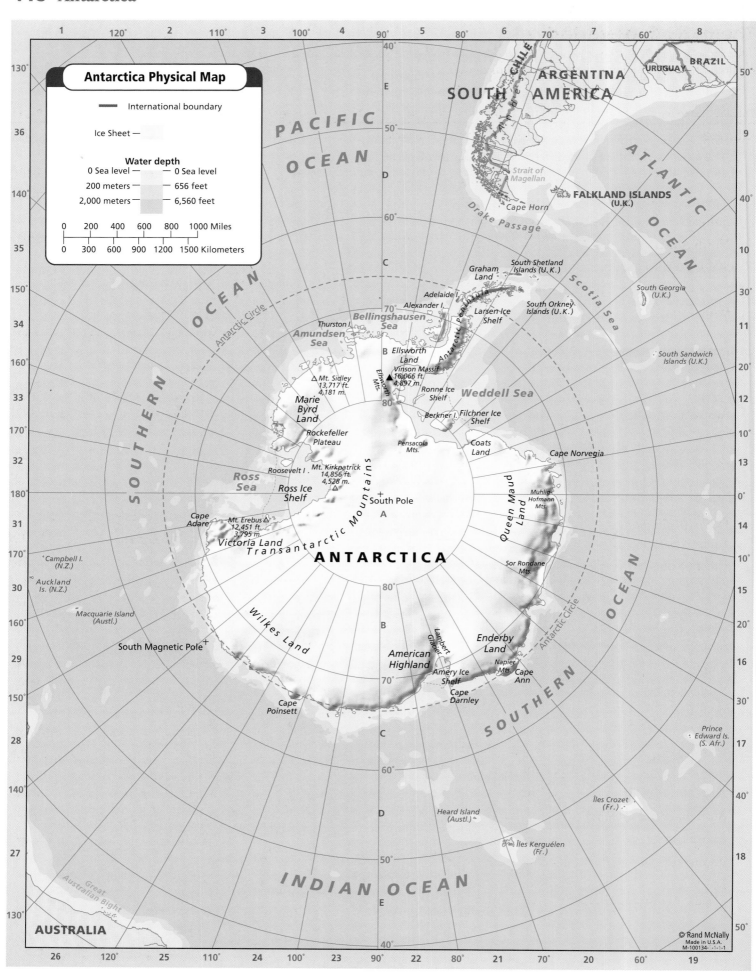

Antarctica Physical Map

— International boundary

Ice Sheet —

Water depth

0 Sea level —	— 0 Sea level
200 meters —	— 656 feet
2,000 meters —	— 6,560 feet

0 200 400 600 800 1000 Miles
0 300 600 900 1200 1500 Kilometers

PACIFIC OCEAN

SOUTHERN OCEAN

Antarctic Circle

SOUTH AMERICA

ARGENTINA
CHILE
URUGUAY
BRAZIL

Strait of Magellan

Drake Passage

Cape Horn

FALKLAND ISLANDS (U.K.)

ATLANTIC OCEAN

South Georgia (U.K.)

Scotia Sea

South Shetland Islands (U.K.)

Graham Land

Adelaide I.

Alexander I.

South Orkney Islands (U.K.)

South Sandwich Islands (U.K.)

Larsen Ice Shelf

Antarctic Peninsula

Thurston I.

Bellingshausen Sea

Amundsen Sea

Ellsworth Land

Vinson Massif 16,066 ft. 4,897 m.

Ronne Ice Shelf

Weddell Sea

△ Mt. Sidley 13,717 ft. 4,181 m.

Ellsworth Mts.

Marie Byrd Land

Rockefeller Plateau

Berkner I.

Filchner Ice Shelf

Pensacola Mts.

Coats Land

Cape Norvegia

Roosevelt I.

Mt. Kirkpatrick 14,856 ft. 4,528 m. △

Ross Sea

Ross Ice Shelf

+ South Pole

A

Transantarctic Mountains

Queen Maud Land

Muhlig Hofmann Mts.

Cape Adare

Mt. Erebus △ 12,451 ft. 3,795 m.

Victoria Land

ANTARCTICA

Sor Rondane Mts.

Campbell I. (N.Z.)

Auckland Is. (N.Z.)

South Magnetic Pole +

Wilkes Land

B

Lambert Glacier

Enderby Land

Napier Mts.

Cape Ann

Macquarie Island (Austl.)

American Highland

Amery Ice Shelf

Cape Darnley

Antarctic Circle

SOUTHERN OCEAN

Cape Poinsett

C

Prince Edward Is. (S. Afr.)

Îles Crozet (Fr.)

Heard Island (Austl.)

Îles Kerguélen (Fr.)

Great Australian Bight

INDIAN OCEAN

AUSTRALIA

© Rand McNally
Made in U.S.A.
M-100134- -1-1-1

Thematic Content Index

This index makes it easy to compare different continents and regions of the world in terms of climate, economies, and other major themes covered in the atlas.

Index of Abbreviations

The following abbreviations are used in the index.

Afr.	Africa	dist.	district	Terr.	Territory or Territories
Austr.	Australia	Eur.	Europe	S.A.	South America
cap.	capital	Mex.	Mexico	U.A.E.	United Arab Emirates
Can.	Canada	mts.	mountains	U.K.	United Kingdom
dep.	dependency	N.A.	North America	U.S.	United States

Index

Review "How to Use the Atlas" page 6 for information on using an index.